BAPTISM BY FLAME

10 STEPS TO IGNITE YOUR LIGHT WITHIN

KRISTIN DWAN

REIKI MASTER / BUSINESS COACH FOR HEALERS

ISBN-13: 978-0998838007

ISBN-10: 0998838004

DEDICATION

This book is dedicated to all of the amazing spiritual teachers I have had the honor of knowing in my life, and there are far too many to mention by name here with my thirty years of spiritual seeking I have done up to today.

From world renowned Saints and authors to psychic readers at small bookstores to the spiritual Elders who I have spent hours with, learning about different facets of my current beliefs in God...I thank you.

From the bottom of my heart and soul I honor you, and lift you up that you may teach thousands your beautiful wisdom.

You have made me the spiritual teacher I am today, and for that I am immensely grateful.

I also dedicate this book to the element of fire.

Without the dance we have done in life, I would not be the powerful phoenix I am today.

I would not take back one ounce of pain you gave me, because on the other side of that pain are my power and wisdom.

My constant spiritual growth was ignited by you, and forever you will glow within me and have a huge home in my heart.

Thank you for being an ever-present teacher.

Thank you for burning me alive and awake.

bap·tism

/ˈbapˌtizəm/

Noun

A person's initiation into a particular activity or role, typically one perceived as difficult.

CONTENTS

ACKNOWLEDGMENTS

This book has a life of its own, and started out many different ways, until 18 years later, it has shown me exactly what it wanted to be. Basically I feel this book wrote itself through me, and throughout the years, I have had many people cheer me along the path of self-doubt within writing it.

Without all of the people who read my blogs, and told me that they inspired them, I may never have had the confidence to write something so deep and telling of my shadow as well as my light.

More recently, I have a huge need to thank my Baptism By Flame team, without whom, this book would never be released.

I am eternally grateful to Elisabeth Rossman who self-published this book for me, and helped me tirelessly with web support and marketing.

To Caroline Gutierrez, who brought my cover art ideas to life in a more beautiful way than I even imagined and formatted everything into book form.

To Laura Beck, who spent hours editing, and cheering me on.

To Steph Ritz, who helped me see that this book was meant to be much more than just a memoir.

I feel so lucky to have had all of you on my side during the birthing of this book, which will not only tell my story, but also serve as a tool to help people within the world ignite their light within.

Thank you also, to the amazing Universe for bringing these creative goddesses to me.

INTRODUCTION

HOW TO BEST USE THIS TOOL

My hope in birthing this book is to give you a tool with which to harness your inner phoenix, which is inherent within all of us. The five elements are Earth, Air, Fire, Water and Spirit.

Each of them are important within our very existence on this planet.

I truly believe that each of us are born a child of a specific element, which through the lessons it provides us, brings us closer to Spirit…the fifth element.

I am a child of fire, and have learned painful, crucial and life altering lessons my whole life with its blazing power. The most memorable of which is dying and coming back to life after accidentally burning down my house with a meditation candle.

Fire is not a gentle teacher by any means, but the lessons she teaches are ones of rebirth, purification and strength.

Without burning within the fires, the phoenix would just be a bird.

Use this book as the tool it was meant to be. There are ten chapters, and each chapter takes you on a specific part of my journey with Spirit. At the end of each chapter is a link to get you to exercises for you to utilize your own inner phoenix.

I suggest having a journal with you. You can use it to do the exercises and keep your inner journey notes in one place.

There will be parts you will be burning, in order to release you from them and the energetic ties they have over you. There will also be parts you may want to keep in a place sacred to you, because they introduce you to parts of yourself that you have either forgotten or never dug deeply enough to meet.

My motto in life is, "Go deep or go home!" and I live this within my day-to-day life, my spiritual path and my work as a Reiki Master/Teacher and Business Coach for Healers and Mystics.

The work will go only as deeply as you allow, and I invite you to challenge yourself to embrace the excavation of your buried skeletons so that you may go deeper than ever before. The beauty of digging deeply is that not only are skeletons buried within our psyches, but treasure is buried there, as well. There is much inner strength and wisdom within you that you will uncover within this work.

My other hope is that by hearing my story of losing everything including my ability to walk, and even breathe at one point, inspires you to realize that even the darkest of days has huge lessons for us. Our pain can become our greatest teacher of power, if we allow that lesson in; pain is the gateway to strength.

If there is one thing I learned through all of this is that our "stuff" is not who we are; our past pain and loss do not have to cripple us today and there is much power to be found within peace, especially when you had to fight for it through something traumatic.

Use this book as the tool to access your inner phoenix, who will then be able to fly you past any blockages into the higher realms of existence that are your birthright.

Releasing my past with love.
Sitting within peace with my present.
Welcoming my future with patience.

— Kristin Dwan

CHAPTER 1

THE DARKNESS BEFORE THE FIRE

We are all like the bright moon,
we still have our darker side.

— Kahlil Gibran

As a child I had the deep need to heal the world, which lead to my aspiration to become a psychologist at age eight.

Only when one comes from the depths of darkness can they really truly appreciate the light. Also, only those who have found their way out of their own darkness know the long hard path from the dark to the light.

As a Reiki Master/Teacher, I signed a soul contract this lifetime to use that directional wisdom from the dark to the light in helping those who are lost within their own private darkness.

I have had many teachers on this warrior's journey of life my soul chose this time around, but none of the human teachers could hold a candle to what I have learned through the element of fire taking everything I owned away, and leaving me to fend for myself as I literally fought to survive another day.

I must have been chosen by fire upon birth, because my first word as a child was, "Hot!!!"

I screamed it as I was being burnt by scalding soup that I accidentally spilled on myself.

My whole life I have searched for truth.

I was born into a Catholic family, got baptized within holy water, went to Christian School through 2nd grade, received First Communion, went to catechism, and was almost confirmed.

Looking back on it now, I didn't know who I was as a teenager let alone who God was. How is it that when you're a teenager it is deemed the appropriate time to confirm you into knowing the who, what, where, when, why and how of your Creator?

Through my whole childhood I remember watching the parishioners during the masses. Some had romance novels on their laps they were reading as the priest pontificated at the podium, some were staring off into space and some were literally asleep. As a child, I never understood why these people came week after week if they so obviously did not want to be there.

Mass, I was taught, was a celebration of your faith in God. Why were so many people asleep, literally or figuratively, during these so-called celebrations? It's no surprise that at age six, I came to question the religion I was taught by my parents.

The one thing I never questioned though, was my connection to nature.

I distinctly remember going from tree to tree in my parent's backyard with a huge coffee can filled with water collecting different leaves, flowers and small rocks to create "Fairy Soup" which I would then sit at the base of the towering avocado tree and serve my friends of the Fae realm.

I also took fondly to the small frogs that lived under the camellia bushes, and would pet them even though my mom would warn me that they could give me warts; I did not care.

Some girls played with Barbies; I played with frogs and fairies.

When I was old enough to learn how to open the sliding glass door on my own, I would go outside with my pillow and blanket and recline on the chaise lounge. I'd stare up at the moon until my eyes closed in sweet slumber.

Sometimes I would even sleep with my eyes open under the moon. I suppose that was my first childhood bout with meditation before I even knew what meditation was.

Places I loved to meditate as a child were under the moon, with the frogs and fairies, and right in front of the fireplace when my parents made a fire.

Fire, and the spirituality within nature, came in equal doses to me as a child, both waltzing in and out: taking turns teaching me and showing me their strength. A waltz that would never end.

Fire is erratic as it is powerful, and I learned that early in life.

My first experience watching a fire burn out of control was when I was at the tender age of six. I noticed my favorite jack-o-lantern, which I named Harvey was smoking up a storm on the fireplace stoop. My parents were busy playing cards with another couple in the other room.

I spent a lot of time alone as an only child, so I made friends with plants, animals and trees, and I used to sit and sing to Harvey when my parents were busy with adult stuff. Next thing I knew, Harvey was doing much more than just smoking. He was sizzling, crackling and singing back to me! The flame that was once the source of golden glow within Harvey was quickly consuming my orange friend.

I sang and watched Harvey burn as if in a trance, when suddenly, the "Fight or Flight" of a six-year-old kicked in, and I screamed, "Daddy, Harvey is on fire!!!"

Of course, my father has no idea who Harvey was, but when he ran into the room to see what was happening, he got some water, and drowned poor sizzling Harvey, until he was nothing more than a black mass of burnt pumpkin in a pool of water.

This would later prove to not be my only dance with fire, but it was my first loss by its flames. It awoke within me a need to experience more of its magical dance.

Around age nine I started really being affected by the phases of the moon. During the Full Moons, I would sneak outside and sleep on the same reclining lawn chairs in the backyard. I would lay there staring at the moon, wide-eyed and completely connected to her energy. I would talk to her, and tell her about stuff that scared me, or things I wanted to bring into my life.

Even at age nine, I knew and understood what being connected to a higher power was. What I sensed lacking in my church, I felt in spades within my mom's backyard with the silvery light of the moon blazing down on me.

I started to feel and celebrate nature more and more as I grew older. Especially the moon and all of the energies I felt around me. Being an only child, I had a lot of time by myself.

Even though I had friends around me, and my friends became like brothers and sisters, I was always OK playing on my own. I never felt alone as a child, because I always felt connected to nature.

I was claimed by the redwood forest as a child of those ancient giants around this time, as well. My mother is a twin, and her twin lives in Humboldt County, CA, surrounded by amazing redwood trees for acres and acres. We would visit often, and I'd very much look forward to spending time in my forest playground.

As a child, I remember running down redwood paths, playing in the filtered sunlight of the forests, tip toeing through beds of mossy clover and hiding within the hollowed out trunks of these mighty beings.

Redwoods are the tallest and one of the oldest living organisms on this planet. It is impossible to see the tops of these trees from the ground. All you see is a seemingly endless reddish brown trunk wider than most cars.

Sprouting from the gigantic trunks is a ceiling of beautiful vibrant green redwood needles; sheltering anyone who finds themselves lucky enough to be within this womb of nature.

The older growth of these trees were around before the Bible was written, before plastic, concrete and steel hit the scene, and before humans completely lost their connection to the earth in order to bind themselves to religions and the rule books that govern their relationship with God.

I remember digging my hands into the moist earth and crying because I did not want to leave to go home to Southern California. I always felt more connected to the Northern way of living even at that young age, and even more so in adulthood.

Once a year, I visit Trinidad, California, a magical fairyland where the forest meets the sea, to do my healing work for the beautiful Humboldt County community.

As an adult I still shed tears on my last day within Humboldt County as I take the sad trip South on the 101 away from my redwood solace.

My happiest and most connected to Spirit moments have been within those forests and the rocky cliffs and shorelines that are married to them. I have a special tree that I found as a teenager on a hike, and promised this mighty giant that I would come visit her every time I was in Humboldt.

Decades later, I have yet to miss a chance to see her every time I am in the area.

This tree is amazing. One of the Ancients. She has a trunk as large as an apartment in San Francisco. Thousands of years ago she was struck by lightning and caught on fire. You can tell this by the hollowed out cave within her trunk. She was burning, but redwoods are so resilient that they can live through being on fire, even near their delicate root system.

Once the fire lost its claim to this mighty being and burned out, the tree remained standing tall with but a hole in its trunk big enough to park a car in where the fire once was. I travel to my tree with pillows, blankets, books, writing supplies, stones and tarot cards in order to connect the closest to my Creator that I know how.

The tops of redwood trees are the closest living things to the heavens. The old growth trees are taller than the Statue of Liberty and whisper the prayers of mankind to the heavens. Within my tree I meditate, write lists, sob, sing and listen.

On my more recent visits, I have been in a very strong place, and not needing to cry and dump all of my emotional baggage into the tree. Instead, I calmly walk into her and give her back a sliver of the decades of healing she has given me by giving her Reiki.

Reiki is energy healing that does not just work wonders on humans, but plants and animals as well. It is Universal Life Energy which flows through all living beings.

During one trip many years ago, I sat on the ground within her and put my arms to each side of me and held the inner walls of her trunk and let the energy flow to her.

I can't even explain in mere words how that energy felt. I was connected to the source of all creation that day. I was calm, strong and elevated beyond any material worries or egotistical desires. I needed nothing and lacked nothing. Being within that tree was everything I ever needed or desired at that moment.

After giving my Nature Mother some Reiki, I said out loud, "Please help me with The Healing Woods. What do I need to do to grow it?"

The Healing Woods is my Reiki Master Coaching practice where I take all that I have learned through schooling and through healing myself from the constant medical trials I have been put though, in order to support others on their paths to healing.

I chose to name it The Healing Woods because of how healing these redwoods have been for me. If it wasn't for my yearly hermitages into the woods, I don't want to know who I might have grown to be, or if I would have even grown. I may have just festered and existed within life in utter darkness.

The moment I asked for help with growing The Healing Woods, my cell phone rang. I did not know the number, and it was that perfect timing that immediately told me it was God calling, and I should definitely answer. When I answered, a female voice on the other side said, "Yes, is this the owner of The Healing Woods? I am calling to help you with your online presence to help you grow your business."

At that moment, I had actual worldly proof that God was listening, and that my tree was a spiritual microphone which amplified my thoughts, dreams, wishes and prayers directly to my Creator's ears.

This tree lived through being on fire, as did I. We were meant to be together, so every year since she first called me to her, I have come to visit her. I feel as though I am somehow connected to this tree from many lives past. She is thousands of years old. Surely we have met before. She is my temple, my church, my meditation hut, my Nature Mother.

I have my Biological Mother who I love dearly, my Nature Mother who is this beautiful tree, and my Spiritual Mother who is Ammachi, the Indian Hugging Saint. I am one lucky girl in the mother department this lifetime, and thank God for all three of them daily.

For two decades, there hasn't been a visit that I haven't come to my tree to meditate. Usually in my 20s and early 30s, I came crying, crawling into it, exploding into screams and sobs, and releasing all of the emotions I had kept hidden inside of me for so long.

Lately, my visits have been to recharge silently, and to give back to her and the earth by offering Reiki to her.

This definitely speaks of the spiritual and emotional growth this amazing being and Reiki have coddled me through.

Around age 11, I experienced my first actual burn from the element of fire.

I was what they called a "Latch Key Kid" in the 80s. Around this time, my parents were divorced, and my mom was working three jobs in order to make ends meet.

In the mornings, my mom would drop me off at my loving grandparents' house. They are the people who taught me love can actually work, and that two people can hold a marriage together "till death do us part."

My grandmother would make me breakfast, and my grandfather

would drive me to school. Some evenings, I would spend the night at their house if my mom went on a trip, or wouldn't be home until late.

This was one of those nights, and I remember my grandparents sitting in their chairs watching *Hee Haw;* my grandmother praying her beautiful green glass rosary and my grandfather asleep with a newspaper on his knees.

I wanted an evening snack, and decided to make instant oatmeal for myself. They had a gas range, and so I turned the flames on high to boil water for my oatmeal.

To this day, I do not know why I used a paper towel to grab the handle of the pot, which was really hot. I guess I was still focused on what was happening on *Hee Haw*, so I forgot to turn the gas burner off before I picked up the pot handle with the paper towel.

Within a second, I felt the intense sting of the fire, and I dropped the pot back on the stove, and the burning paper towel in the water. My fingers burned and pulsed like I had never felt, and I immediately put them in cold water and went about my business.

I'm not sure why I never told anyone about it. I suppose it was because I knew I would be OK once the burning subsided. My fingers were red, but no broken skin, so I just kept the incident to myself, and went on making my oatmeal.

I do remember the burns taking a while to heal, but they were on the inside of my hand, so it was easy to conceal. I suppose I learned early on to conceal my pain, especially the emotional pain, but this time, it was the physical pain I hid with a smile.

I was always a class clown, yet also a nerd by the cool kids' standards because I was in advanced classes. Little did they know, I was hiding astronomical amounts of pain beneath my armor of laughter and black clothes.

As my inner turmoil grew, so did my desire to connect to the spirit world, perhaps to escape the pain happening on the earthly realm.

It was on my first railroad track experience that I met one of my spirit guides for the first time.

I was around 14 years old, and hanging out with some older girls I met in high school. They were on their way out as seniors while I had just begun my high school journey as a freshman, so of course I had to prove myself worthy of hanging out with the older tribe.

They hung out at the railroad tracks under a bridge, and I was intrigued because the local shopping center was the only hangout spot I knew back then. I remember the huge sense of excitement as we took the tracks on our bikes and rode to the bridge. They taught me how to sense if a train was coming by putting a penny on the tracks and also taught me about the traffic light off in the distance of the tracks. If it was shining red, that meant a train would be coming any minute.

The train track warning light turned from green to yellow, and my excitement soared in time with my adrenaline! We ditched our bikes under the bridge near some hobo's leavings and the girls said, "Are you ready to play chicken? You've done it before, right?"

Of course I had not! I didn't even know railroad tracks were a place to hang out until this day, but I had to prove myself, and said, "Yeah I have, millions of times. Let's go!"

We climbed up onto the tracks, and I heard one of the girls yell, "RED!!!" like a warrior, and we all screamed out like a pack of wolves. I heard the wailing of the train horn in the distance just before I saw the one-eyed beast charging at us, around the corner a mile or so down the tracks.

Now, I don't know if you have ever been staring a locomotive down as it hurtles towards you at 60 miles an hour while you are standing in the middle of the train tracks, but the amount of noise is deafening and the wind it creates can easily knock you down. To 14-year-old me, who had no idea what she was doing, it was completely overwhelming.

My mind went blank.

I forgot where I was, and I forgot that the whole point of my existence at that moment was to jump off the tracks before the one eyed goliath monster of machinery squashed me like a watermelon.

The train came closer and all of a sudden the screaming of the horn, pounding of the wheels and the screams of my friends telling me to get off the tracks cut to silence.

I heard nothing except the sound of a male voice within my head saying, "Get off the tracks. Get off the tracks right now!"

The only people anywhere near us were my friends, and they were all female. There were no males anywhere around. Just as his voice yelled "Right now!" my body was physically thrown off the tracks seconds before the train came roaring through the spot I once occupied.

This brought up many questions for me. A few being, "Am I

crazy and hearing voices?" "Was that my Guardian Angel?" and the most life changing, "Who do I turn to in order to find out?"

Soon after, I met my first witch, Mary. She was more than happy to answer these questions for me.

She was older than I...at least 20 years old, and she was the first person I trusted to tell my whole story to after the first couple friends I told laughed and called me crazy.

As soon as she heard it, she nodded knowingly, and told me I had just met one of my spirit guides.

This lead to me needing to get to know who they are, what they look like and what their names are. Mary gave me my first lesson in candle magic. She told me to anoint the candle with my spit, carve a question mark in it and sit and meditate with it asking the spirit guide who helped me with the train to tell me his name.

I did this with conviction every night for weeks, and sat there staring at the candle for hours each night. I would do tarot readings on myself all night long by the light of my question mark candle, asking the cards to give me an idea of whom from the spirit realm it was that saved me from sudden death by train that fateful day.

One night, as I was meditating on my candle, I slipped into another dimension. I'm not sure if it was the hot summer night, the incense, Siouxsie and The Banshees playing in the background or a combination of all three, but whatever it was, I was finding myself caught between two worlds, and had my first deep out of body meditation.

I saw a figure of light grow from a tiny dot the size of a cherry into a human sized form in front of me, and I felt no fear, only complete and utter trust and love.

Wordlessly he spoke to me, and somehow, even though my ears were not physically hearing the voice outside of my head, I recognized his voice as the voice I heard on the train tracks right before my body was thrown from the path of the train.

I sensed a smile come from him, though I did not see his face. He reached out to me and embraced me, and I felt as if I was flying high up in the sky. For some time I remember flying with my new spirit friend, and feeling the wind against my face and the highs and lows as we soared through the meditative sky I was in.

Once our adventure was over, I again sensed a smile from him, and as his full human form slowly dissolved, I was left with the name, Indiad.

Indiad. After months of meditation and seeking, I had finally met my first spirit guide, and knew his name. Indiad.

I was elated, and immediately replaced the question marks that I carved into my candles with "Indiad."

I thanked him for saving me, and continued to ask him for help in tarot readings, and with life in general. If I had a hard test coming up, and I was worried about it, I asked for help from him, and felt his energy come around me as I took the test, and usually ended up breezing through the answers to get a better grade than I expected

My first introduction to tarot cards came just before I met Indiad. I felt an instant connection, one that I still to this day nurture.

I never even had a reading, but knew I had to be a Tarot reader the moment I laid eyes upon the Ryder-Waite deck in the B Dalton "Occult" section. I would visit incessantly and spend all of my baby-sitting and allowance money on books about Wicca, meditation and spirituality there.

Most girls were buying music, clothes and makeup, while I was saving my pennies for the latest book on spell casting, meditation or tarot.

I was also a gothic/death rock kid. I wore black capes, black lipstick and spider web lace skirts that I hand sewn myself. I hung out with the nerds, cast outs, punks and misfits. In our group, there were skaters, punks, heshers and loadies.

I was always advanced in school, so I was in classes with pretty much the same kids from grade three through high school, and had beautiful friendships, some of which I still enjoy to this day.

I sat in class with the nerds and geeks and went to lunch and recess with the misfits and punks. I belonged nowhere, yet I could make myself right at home anywhere. Something I still enjoy to this day; the makings of a true gypsy.

I did tarot readings for kids in the school library during lunch.

I always found it funny that a cheerleader, a nerd and chola would all be in line to get a reading from the goth. Once they sat down, all boundaries were lost, and I connected with them, and told them what I saw. Through what I saw, we spoke and got to know each other, and once the reading was over, I understood them a lot better, and they accepted me more underneath the armor of black lipstick and black lace veils.

I came into 9th grade onto the grounds of Monrovia High School a scared little fish in a big ocean trying to find a group to hide in for protection from the normal kids. I graduated having friends within every group, with a new understanding of myself, and how to have connective conversations with all different types of people, as well as a growing love of the occult and divination.

I noticed that when I used Indiad for tarot readings, I started to be able to see and hear the messages instead of merely reading the cards. I started to just open my mouth and talk, not thinking about the words that were coming out; almost a stream of consciousness that I hoped made sense to the questioner. More often than not, it did, and my reputation as a tarot reader spread like wildfire on campus.

I heard Indiad's guidance more clearly and loudly the more I worked with him within my readings. After a while, I started to work with him in meditations, as well. I wanted to be able to speak with him without needing to rely on the tarot cards. I wanted a direct connection to the spirit realm, and I wanted it now.

When my mother first found my tarot cards, she did not take too well to them. In fact, she was not taking too well to the black clothes, black flowers in my room, gothic music constantly surrounding me — especially The Cure. I could listen to Robert Smith sing all hours I was awake back then — and she especially didn't appreciate her daughter ditching catechism, saying she does not believe in God, and now having tarot cards in her room.

My mother grew up in Torrington, Connecticut and is very proper and not interested in rocking the boat or sticking out from normal society. To have this gothic daughter studying witchcraft and ditching her catechism classes was just a bit too much for the woman who grew up in a small town in New England.

She threw them away, asked if I was worshipping the devil, and forced me to go see the priest who baptized me thinking that it would somehow remind me of the spirituality I had lost. What she didn't realize is that even as a child I never found it in the beautifully ornate stained glass walls of Annunciation Church in Arcadia. It was never there for me to find, nor lose for that matter.

My mother drove a 15-year-old me to the church, and we met with Father Zimmerman. He was a jovial old priest who held me as a baby and dunked my head into the holy water, therefore pronouncing me Catholic and on the path to finding God before my first birthday.

I remember sitting with Father Zimmerman, and he tried to make things as comfortable as possible with pleasantries, and then he went in for the kill by asking if I believed in God. I said that I did not because I have no proof he exists.

To this he went on a long flowery sermon about how faith is what brings the soul to "see" God and faith is the only proof we as Catholics need in order to believe in God. He closed with the following, which I will never forget, "God is like the wind. We can't see the wind, but we know it is there."

He watched my face after he finished, and I looked right back into his eyes, and said, "Well I can hear the wind as it blows through the trees and I feel it blow on my face and move my hair around. I cannot, however, feel your God."

At this, Father Zimmerman slowly shook his head in sadness, and could not say much more to me. My mind had been made up. I did not believe in God.

At the same time I was arguing God and spirituality with my mother and priests, I was also schooling myself on all of the different religions out there. Since this is pre-Google era, I would ride my bike over to the library and occult bookstores to look up any and all different types of religions I knew about at that point. I studied Zen, Buddhism, Wicca, Kabbalah, Hinduism and I even read the Necronomicon and The Satanic Bible just because I wanted to learn what it is they believe before making the decision that I do not believe it.

My mother continued driving me to catechism every week, and I continued to ditch and go to the field of the school next door and sit under trees. I'd write poetry, meditate and do tarot readings in the grass for myself to practice my craft.

There finally came a time when the church told my mom I was not able to be confirmed with the rest of my class, because I had been absent so much, and at that point I think the realization hit that it was time for her to give up, and that I had made my own decision on what and who I did and didn't believe in.

My hatred of God was not in full bloom yet. More the hatred of myself was being nurtured at age 15. I was an only child of divorce, had an alcoholic father and a very controlling mother. I emotionally ate and have had a lifelong battle with my weight.

I suppose I felt that I didn't have control over anything in my life, so I chose to eat all I could because I had the fear that people would leave, or I could not control any other situations in my life, so

I controlled how much I emotionally ate — a lot of food, and often.

I suppose, now that I look back on me becoming a Goth, it was not only being drawn to the melancholy dark tones of the music which complimented my mood at the time, but it was also an armor to keep people away, and to redirect the kids' harsh judgments of me to my clothes instead of the body inside the clothes.

It hurt less when they yelled, "Are you a vampire for Halloween?" or "Who died? Are you going to a funeral?" or my personal favorite, "Beetlejuice, Beetlejuice, Beetlejuice!" as I walked down the hallway.

These ridiculous things hurt way less than being called fat, nerd or ugly. The weirder my armor got, the less they noticed the body and louder they yelled about the armor. Which was just fine with me.

All teenagers are awkward and not comfortable in their skin. Hormones are raging and ideas about who they are, what the world is and what their place is in it are battling any type of sense of peace and calm within.

My outlets for the emotional war inside of me when I was away from the redwoods were writing poetry, reading about different religions, listening to music full blast on my Walkman and cutting on and burning myself.

The stress had built up within me so intensely that no longer did painting and drawing work to relieve it. Instead I began taking a safety pin and scratching words and images into my skin until it bled.

I also clicked on lighters for minutes at a time, so their metal tips became extremely hot, and burned myself with them. Another favorite was pouring hot wax on my skin, and playing with a candle's flame as it burned. I learned how to make a candle drip fire, and on more than one occasion, I dripped small amounts of flaming wax on myself just to feel alive.

At this point in life, I was feeling emotionally dead inside. The only feeling I had inside was anger. The endorphins from the cuts and burns gave me a high that drained the anger out, and left me feeling a release.

Only problem was, those means of releasing anger only worked for a short amount of time, and like any addict with her medicine, I kept needing more.

One day in particular, I was feeling completely hopeless about my 15 year old life, and I distinctly remember making a plan to jump into my mom's pool, and tie myself onto a huge boulder that would sink me to the bottom. Don't ask me where I was going to get the boulder, or how I would get it to the pool. I didn't plan it out that well. I was focused on the outcome only.

I also had plans to mix bleach and vinegar, which created a poisonous fume that made it impossible to breathe in a closed area such as my closet. I also learned about being in a closed garage with a car running for a long time in order to end it all.

All of these took far too much planning, and were pretty much impossible to do while living with my mother, so I took the easy way out, and took a pink plastic Daisy shaver, and went to town on my wrists.

Now, obviously we all know that using a pre-teen's pink plastic shaving device is not going to kill anyone, but the desire was there, even though the tool was ridiculous.

I had "Siamese Twins" by The Cure playing in my room. Robert Smith's tortured voice singing over and over, "Is it always like this?!" intertwined with drum and bass that spoke of funeral dirges of primal historic times.

I chose this song to slit my wrists to when I decided that it would be a good idea to take my own life. This was before CD players, so I made it my day's work to create a tape of the song playing over and over and over again using my double tape recorder, so I could hear the song as I drifted off into the eternal darkness.

I didn't drift into eternal darkness. At all.

In fact I barely felt a thing from the pink Daisy shaver.

It did, however leave lots of nasty red cuts on my wrists for a teacher to see at school the next day, and immediately my mom was called out of work to come pick up her suicidal daughter from school.

This attempt was the last straw for my mom in a long line of battles that proved to her that she had completely lost control of her daughter.

I was sneaking out multiple times a week, even though my bedroom door was taken off the hinges to promote my staying put. I was cutting on myself and burning myself almost daily, and even though I felt so out of control of my own life, I can only now imagine how out of control my poor mother felt, not knowing what her depressed and suicidal goth daughter would do next.

The only thing that made sense to her to happen next was for me to be put in Las Encinas Hospital, in the youth unit with a bunch of drug users, gang members and severely depressed kids my age.

Notice how I never once mentioned drugs in the past pages? That is because there never had been any. I didn't even smoke cigarettes or have my first drink until after I was released from that prison.

A nerd of a goth girl with red marks on her wrists from a pink plastic Daisy razor was cast into the snake pit of Las Encinas, and she had to fit in with the natives, or else it would not be pretty.

I smoked my first cigarette in the hospital, got into my first physical fight, pierced my own nose with a safety pin, took my first prescription drugs and climbed my first 14-foot fence as I went AWOL with another patient one Sunday Family Picnic Day.

I now realize that the mental hospital stay alone could be its own memoir, and perhaps one day it will, but I will just say that I am glad in the long run that it happened.

When you are put into one of those as a kid, shit gets real rather quickly, and the only way that I was going to be released was if I played by the rules and went through all of the levels of work they gave us to do.

Obviously with a physical fight and going AWOL on my record, my stay was much longer than expected, with a nice ambulance ride to a high-security hospital named CPC in Alhambra.

Getting put into CPC made Las Encinas seem like a country club.

I was literally in there with a Crip and a Blood - two of the most famous rival gangs in Los Angeles, and even they had to get along and work together in order to get out. When you are a teenager in a psych ward, it is you against the establishment. All of us had to ban together in order to get the sign offs we needed to be released.

This lovely three month stay over one summer really opened my eyes to how good my life actually was. I was in there with gang members, kids who had been sexually abused their whole lives, kids on large amounts of drugs, one who was mute and one who suffered from multiple personalities.

All of a sudden, my divorced parents, misunderstood spirituality and way of dress didn't seem as bad as it did before, and the cutting and burning of myself stopped, but the drinking and smoking began.

They were the new coping tools I learned during my summer jaunt in the mental ward.

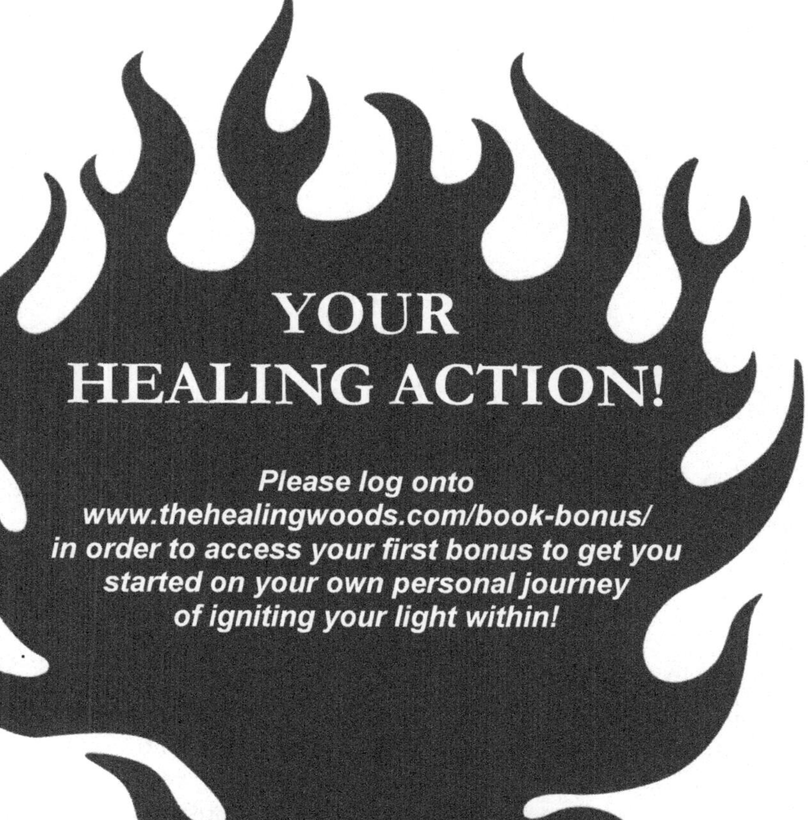
YOUR
HEALING ACTION!
Please log onto
www.thehealingwoods.com/book-bonus/
in order to access your first bonus to get you
started on your own personal journey
of igniting your light within!

CHAPTER 2

REBIRTHDAY

The phoenix must burn to emerge.

—Janet Fitch

When I graduated from high school at 17 and moved out on my own the very next day, my life was a blur of parties, bad decisions and depression. I was a sort of gypsy traveling from house to house, room to room and apartment to apartment every year or so.

I was either moving in with a boyfriend, breaking up with said boyfriend, then moving in with random friends until I settled for a couple years in the house.

This house would prove to be the cave I would suffer my darkest of depressions in until I ended up accidentally burning down the house in order to escape my self-inflicted torture.

On the surface, my six roommates and I looked like we were having the best time ever and our house was always the party destination spot for countless people ranging from the ages of 15 to late 30s. LA punk scene, Cacophony Society folks, local bands, 90s Goth scene hierarchy, you name it…those walls gladly received them.

Every time I came home from my job managing a JoAnne's Fabrics and Crafts store, I was welcomed by at least 10 friends either offering laughs, communally cooked dinners, invites to go drinking

or tables full of drugs.

It was the perfect place for me to completely ignore the growing depression and hatred of myself, of God, love, and of life in general.

There was always a band to go see in the local music scene. Sometimes they even practiced in our living room. Always a drama to witness or create and always something more exciting to experience than to deal with was really going on inside me.

That house could end up being a whole memoir on its own as well. So many characters. So many adventures. So many stories contained within those burned down walls.

I was suffering through it all with a growing pit of sadness within me. I scaled the lower walls of my deep dark well of emotion. I never let myself completely fall to the bottom of it by writing in my journals, losing myself in music, dancing at Goth clubs four nights a week, doing Full Moon ceremonies and meditative candle work whenever I felt things were getting really intense within the well.

Even though I chose to lose myself most times, there was always a search for truth happening hidden very deeply within me. Once I hit my early 20s, I decided I was going to search for what that truth for me was at that tumultuous time; countless journal entries were written within that search.

The one that stands out the most was written during a night spent on mushrooms, a few nights before the fire. It closed with the following self-fulfilling proclamation, "I feel as if I am at a stale point in life…I need change…I need a push. I can't deal with this pain any longer. I can't handle the stagnation I am suffering through. When will life change? When will I be released? When will I be pushed off the ledge of fear and depression into the arms of change and be directly connected to whatever is out there pulling my strings?"

Little did I know that with all of the seeking I did for some sort of direct connection outside of me, the connection was within me the whole time. I just had no idea how to access it until my chaotic connection with life as I knew it was cut off completely.

The reset button of my life was about to be pressed, and I had no idea what a baptism by flame I was in for as I suffered silently within my darkness, hate, fear and depression.

I had just received a promotion to store manager at JoAnn fabrics, so I went to celebrate by buying myself a huge bag full of new clothes for my new job title.

I was severely depressed at this point in my life too, so celebrating by buying myself something was a way to put off my true emotions from coming to the surface and instead, buy something to dress up the walls that hid what was really going on beneath the skin.

I went to visit my friend Amber when the trifecta of accidental growth began.

In the middle of our visit there was a huge crash outside her door where my car was parked.

We ran outside to see what it was, and saw our friend and her neighbor Damani standing near my car apologizing profusely for backing into it.

There was no visible damage, so we all laughed it off and I was on my way to go home, to hang my brand new clothes up for my first day of work.

That's when the second of three accidents that weekend reared its ugly head.

I pulled up next to a double semi-truck, and stopped at the red light to see if there was any oncoming traffic before I made my right turn.

Just as I stopped, the semi started to turn right, directly in front of me. I panicked and closed my eyes, gripped the steering wheel and pressed down with superhuman strength upon the brake pedal, as if it would somehow make the semi stop literally running over my car.

I watched in shock as the first trailer scraped the front end of my car and shook it uncontrollably.

When the first trailer finished its attack on the fortress of my little tiny Honda CRX 2 door hatchback, the grand finale of the second trailer made its presence known.

First it made contact with my driver's side door, almost ripping it off, and then continued scraping the entire side of my car before it literally ran over the hood of my car on its way down the street.

I was in complete and utter silent shock. I could not believe that A – my tiny Honda CRX two-door hatchback had just been literally run over by a double semi, and that B – I was still alive within it, watching my attacker ramble away further down the road of life.

Even though my car had been run over and one tire was flat, I was somehow able to drive it enough to catch up to the semi-truck driver stopped at the next red light, who had no idea the truck he was driving ran over a vehicle.

I got out of my car and flagged him down screaming, "You hit me!!!!"

I will never forget the look of shock and anger on his face as he pulled over, and got out of his truck to look at my car.

We had to pull over in a parking lot in order to accommodate the double trailer, and the first thing he says to me as he jumps out of his truck is, "I just have to say one thing right now. You people in small cars need to watch out for trucks!"

"Shouldn't it be the other way around?" I asked. The cops were called.

There were no witnesses that stayed for either side, but he did not have his right turn signal on in the middle lane of the previous intersection, which is why I assumed he was going straight, so it was OK for me to go into the right turn lane to make a right turn. Little did I know that Karma had other plans for us.

There was a huge heat wave in Pasadena on August 22nd, 1998, which was, in hindsight, a foreshadowing of the literal fire to come into my life later that night.

I called a tow truck, and had the three-wheeled remains of my car towed to my house. I walked in the door, and vented all about the accident to my roommate Orestes, to which he said, "You need to escape this bullshit for a while, and go to Al's Bar with me. Cuba Las Vegas is playing."

Al's Bar was a seedy pre-gentrified Downtown LA punk haven with graffiti covered walls, probably the worst bathrooms in any public establishment and beer served in huge red plastic cups. It was like going to a house party on the set of Suburbia, and just what I needed to forget my troubles that day.

When I got home from a night of rock and roll, friends, and forgetting the dejected pile of metal my car was reduced to, I retreated to the safe haven of my room, and drifted off to a fitful sleep. I awoke screaming from a nightmare of a semi-truck on fire barreling down a mountain straight for me, and thus…my baptism began.

I shuddered in bed remembering the images tearing through my head seconds ago, and wanted to take some time to read to get my mind off of them before attempting sleep again.

My ankle had been hurting since the accident. I suppose with the amount of superhuman strength I was pushing down my brake pedal while the semi crawled over my car had somehow tweaked my ankle.

Instead of walking across the room to turn on the light, I lit my Road Opening candle near my bed, read a couple of pages and accidentally drifted off to sleep while the candle went blazing through all I owned and began my dance with fire and death.

The irony that a Road Opener candle started the fire was not lost on me. In Wicca and Roots Magic, a Road Opener candle is burned when you need a change in life or luck. It gets rid of any blockages that stand in between you and success.

Little did I know, life as I knew it was what was about to be taken out of my way completely.

The next thing I know, I hear my cat Lydia screaming at me, and clawing my face. Before I could even get upset about it, I felt the heat near my head, opened my sleepy eyes and looked just above me to see the curtains inches from my pillow raging in flames. Just as I shot up from the pillow, those very curtains fell onto that same pillow, which was overtaken by fire within seconds.

I started screaming, "OH MY GOD!!! OH MY GOD!!!" over and over as I quickly lost control of the erratic wall of flames taking over my bedroom.

Many years later, as I look back upon on my choice of words that I screamed at age 23, I find it funny that I was calling out to God even though at the time I hated Him.

Little did I know that those flames leaving me with 3rd degree burns over 30-percent of my body would act as a baptism for me, and start me on a long journey of finding out who God was to me and how I could learn to accept and love Him as an adult.

I went into fight or flight mode, and unfortunately I decided to fight. If flight would have been my choice, I would not be writing quite the same book I am writing today.

My whole life I have never been one to run away from experiencing the pain of a lesson. I have never been one to read about lessons or be taught lessons. I have to feel them, experience them, and literally be burnt alive by them in order to internalize what it is I am supposed to learn.

Some would find this foolish, but I do find that all the lessons I have felt, have buried deep seeds of wisdom within me that are constantly evolving and changing me.

Better to have seeds of wisdom buried where the holes from skeletons being exhumed remain.

Instead of running out of the house, and waiting for the fire department to fight the fire which was quickly taking over my room and house, I decided to grab a small waste paper basket I had in my room, and run down the hall to the bathroom and fight the quickly growing fire storm within my room.

Our house was very old, and had plumbing from the 20s, so the water was at best a fast trickle, and filling the trash can took what felt like years, although it was probably only a minute or two.

I ran into the dark hallway, and the doorway to my room was dancing with red, yellow and orange flickering light. Smoke was billowing out the door, and still, I walked in ready to fight the fire barefoot in cut off black velvet leggings and a Cure T-shirt.

I ran into the room and immediately felt the heat of the fire like running into a wall. By this point, my bed was completely engulfed in flames, as was the dresser and nightstand next to it.

I took the sad amount of water I had within the trashcan and just flung the whole thing into the heart of the fire. The wall of flames almost laughed at me while crackling and jumping out towards me and singeing my eyebrows, bangs and eyelashes off.

Fire is very erratic with its movements. It has a crazy dance it does, and this fire was growing in size, strength and temperature by the second. It took on a life of its own, and I felt as if I was being followed and watched as I moved about the room trying to fight it, all the while screaming, "OH MY GOD!" over and over again.

I didn't even notice the huge burns all over my bare feet, thighs, arms and hands…I was too busy fighting a losing battle with the element of fire, and losing track of time and myself within the smoke, heat and power of the angry inferno my room had become.

I finally got out of the room, by running through a dancing wall of flames with my bare feet, and blindly ran outside to sit in the middle of the street rocking and crying at four in the morning, watching as if in a dream, as the firemen arrived and started fighting the lesson I had created. I was saying over and over again, "Why isn't it out yet?" and "Why is this happening to me?" over and over and over again.

In what seemed like weeks, but was probably around an hour…the flames were finally out, and the firemen had put a huge flood light in the room to make sure all of the embers were out.

I will never forget the site of what once was my room being this huge opaque black hole, shining brightly within the still dark backdrop of the early morning sky. It was almost as if the Universe was putting a spotlight on my lesson and what I thought at that moment was my biggest defeat in life yet.

The sound of water dripping, the sizzling and settling of the injured house and the sight of firemen shoveling all the burnt rubble that was my lifetime of possessions overtook me, and I finally became aware of the intense burning all over my body.

I was looking down at my fingers, which were all curled up and gnarled with huge white bubbles of skin everywhere. I couldn't get my rings off, which later had to be cut off of me in the ER.

The ambulance driver looked at me, and said, "We need to get you to the ER right now." but I refused because I wanted to stay to make sure all of the animals we had in the house were OK.

My roommates Vivian and Orestes were there, so I figured once I tracked down all of the animals, I could have one of them take me to the ER if needed. I was completely in shock and in denial about the severity of my injuries.

I went into a neighbor's house, and got a glass of water, and used her restroom. It was at that moment that I saw my face, which was black from the smoke, and my singed hair, eyebrows and eyelashes. I washed my face, and burnt hair fell out all over her white sink. I later came over after I was healed, with flowers because I felt bad about how horrible I left her bathroom.

At this point, the sun had risen, and shined a light on the situation, and my room had been gutted by the firemen, and what was left of my burned belongings had been strewn all over the front yard.

I noticed a half burned tarot card right at the entrance to our door.

The Tower Card. It is a card that depicts a tower collapsing in flames with a phoenix flying above it.

The Tower in tarot, is a usually unforeseen catastrophe, illness or change within your life which hurts while you are going through it, but after you move through it, a rebirth takes place, and you come out of it stronger and right where you need to be.

This fire was definitely the biggest Tower I had experienced in my 23 years of life, and at that moment, I had no idea how much my life would be changing, and how strong I would have to fight to survive during it all.

Interestingly enough, the only items of mine that survived the fire were my ten years of paper journals, photo albums and my grandmother's jewelry. How the paper items survived in the black pit of destruction my room had become is seriously still beyond me.

Once all of the animals were accounted for: five cats and one dog, I couldn't take the burning in my hands and feet any longer, and my roommate Vivian drove me to the nearest ER in Glendale, California.

The morning air was brisk, and I had my hands hanging out of the car to cool the constant heat like a hot iron on them down the whole way there.

They admitted me immediately, and had freezing cold water that they kept having me immerse my hands and feet in. Even with them in ice-cold water, I could still feel the searing heat within my tissue as third degree burns continue to damage you as the heat makes its way to muscle and bone. It was the worst on my right foot on my middle toe, which I would later be told may not make it through the skin grafting surgeries.

My hands were burned so badly that I could not get my rings off, and they had to cut them off of me because my fingers were swelled up so badly with huge white bubbly blisters and burns.

Vivian was in the room with me as I was moaning and screaming, covered in freezing cold water and my arms and legs shaking in pain and shock for what seemed like hours.

Once the burns were cooled down enough to release me, they gave me a shot of painkiller, prescription for more and a note saying that I should go immediately to The Grossman Burn Ward.

I was driven to get my Vicodin prescription since I had no car thanks to the battle my Honda lost with the double semi, and then I passed out on a bed within a small part of the house untouched by the flames.

That day was a blur of ambulance chaser insurance suits stopping by, giving me their card and saying, "Sorry for your loss." Red Cross stopped by to give me a voucher for $50 worth of food and $100 worth of clothing, which I gladly accepted because I had no money in the bank. The only clothes I had left were what I slept in the night before, which were tattered and smelling of smoke.

My good friend Jamie was on vacation, and her house was empty, so she invited us all to bring the animals there with her two cats. I was still in complete shock and denial about how bad the burns were, and still had not called my parents to tell them that I was in a fire, almost died and that my appendages were burned to a crisp.

I now see that this was a pattern. Burning myself, and not telling anyone about it, just like when I burned myself at my Grandparents' house, and kept that hidden as well.

This time, however, was proving to be quite impossible to hide.

Orestes, Vivian and I were in Jamie's house watching *The Doors* movie, and I took another Vicodin before falling asleep within the blissful arms of denial knowing full well that the next day, I would have to face the music. I'd have to tell my mother, see how the burns were doing and figure out if I needed to go to the burn ward or not.

The next couple days were literally a blur of pain killers, friends coming to check on me and having to tell my roommates who were on vacation, that when they came back home, there wasn't going to be any home.

My mom stepped in and made the appointment at The Grossman Burn Ward for me, and picked me up and took me in. It had been about three days since the fire, and those bubbles of pus that I was in denial about, thinking they would go away with over the counter burn ointment, had 72 hours now to fester and become completely infected.

There were three types of burns I noticed that I had. Big white puffy blisters, red raw super painful ones and these weird white patches of my skin that were hard and leathery which had no feeling at all.

I remember as Dr. Grossman looked at my white leathery burns, I said, "I can't even feel those. They must not be too bad." To which he said, "I can imagine you aren't feeling those at all. Those are your worst burns, they burned right through your nerves."

It was at that moment that I was told that I needed to come back the next morning for my first of multiple Skin Graft surgeries. There was still a part of me that was in huge denial about it; I had no idea which way was up or down, but the next few weeks would show me my soul, and just how dark things have to get for the will to live and thrive to kick in.

The first step of trying to recover my skin was to take the skin of random cadavers, and use that to graft onto my burns to promote my own skin's healing.

For the month I was in the burn ward, I had a patchwork of different colors and types of skin up and down my arms and legs and on my hands and feet. It looked like the goriest of quilts from your childhood nightmares, and it was my new normal for the time being. That took some time to get used to.

Waking up and looking at them each day brought tears to my

eyes, especially since it appeared that my skin was never going to look normal again. What brought tears to my eyes more so, was the constant feeling of hot irons on the 30-percent of my body that suffered the burns. Even the constant Morphine drip I was on did hardly anything to mask the pain that radiated throughout my whole being.

The first day of my month-long stay started out with a bang. I reacted badly to whatever anesthesia they used to put me under, and my heart stopped. I was completely down for the count, so this part of my journey I am not aware of consciously. There was no white light, no angels guiding me to God and no remembrance at all of the time my heart stopped beating.

I do, however, remember the exact moment I came back to life, and I was much more aware of energies and of the different organs in my body, and how they were slowly waking up from being dead.

I remember being half in and half out of my body, and hearing them talk about me as if I wasn't there. They were very concerned about my blood pressure, and kept monitoring it, and my heart rate.

I remember feeling a sense of compassion for my body that I had never thought to have before leaving it for some time. Our bodies are amazing machines that can take huge beatings, and still bounce back. We really are miracles within a skin jacket. My skin jacket was hanging on by a thread at that moment, but the soul within it was fighting to stay here for me.

This is what it feels to be literally "death warmed over." I had heard that term used many times, but after this day I really felt to my core what it means and how it feels.

For the next 24 hours, it was touch and go, and I was being watched almost non-stop. I was hooked up to monitors, and slept for 20 of those hours. My throat was on fire, because while I was unconscious and reacting to the anesthesia, I threw up and was choking on it as well, so they had to shove a long tube down my throat in order to clear the air passage.

My burns hurt more than ever. What was once a dull yet deep pain underneath the blisters, was now a raw and screaming pain underneath the skin grafted onto me from deceased humans I have never met, but I thank for their contribution to my healing.

It was a good thing I slept so long, because once I woke up, I wanted to do nothing but escape the constant burning, yet there was sadly no escape.

A friend came to visit, and brought me a journal to write in. Even though my hands were covered in burns and bandages, I somehow managed to hold a pen very awkwardly with my thumb and middle finger since the others were wrapped up, and literally scribbled my thoughts about dying and coming back to life.

Even though I was in constant pain, I was excited to be alive, and knew that I was allowed back into this body for a reason. I couldn't wait to get out to start my life over again! The first thing to bring into my life upon getting out into the real world was a band.

My whole life I sang. I sang before I spoke as a child, running around with the fairies. I sang in choirs starting in first grade, and continued all the way through high school. It became my main form of release as I got older and outgrew cutting on myself.

Once I graduated high school, sadly the singing stopped, unless I was with my friends at a dive bar singing Karaoke, which I loved to do often. I lived in a house full of musicians, and whenever anyone heard me sing, they always said, "You need to sing in a band!"

My low self-esteem and fear of being seen kept me on the dingy Karaoke stages singing to my friends and the few other people who happened to be there, and away from sharing my vocal gifts with the world in any real way.

In the Grossman Burn Ward, hours after being reborn, I realized it was time to start a real band. I had no idea how I was going to do it, or who I was going to do it with; I just knew that somehow it was going to happen. A deep inner knowing flooded through me, and I rested within that wisdom. I felt it deep within my bones.

I was so excited to start my new life. I couldn't wait for the skin grafts to be healed enough so I could take flight as the phoenix I knew I was!

Each day I awoke expecting to see some improvement in my skin, and each day I looked, and nothing was changing. In my head I thought that they would magically fade away, and Dr. Grossman would release me to go be the rock star I now knew I could be.

Nothing was further from the truth; in fact, the next time I saw him, he gave me the bad news that the cadaver grafts were not healing like he hoped they would, and we would need to move onto autografts, which meant taking good skin from somewhere on my body, and attaching it to the wounds in order to more powerfully promote healing.

I was immediately frightened to my core. I was not only scared of the new level of pain I would be experiencing on my upper thighs, which were to be the donor sites of the skin to be placed on my hands, arms and feet, but I was also afraid that once I was put under for the surgery, I would never come back.

Interesting that just a few years prior, I was doing research on how to end my life, and now that I was having this second chance after actually losing it, I was scared to death of missing out on this new life.

There wasn't much else I could do in my present situation than trust my surgeon, who told me multiple times that they would not be using the same thing that I reacted so badly to when they put me under. In fact, I would be given an extra medication to calm my nerves and heart an hour prior to the next surgery, which was scheduled for the next morning.

That night I was given something to put me to sleep, but before I drifted off, I did something I hadn't done in over a decade. I prayed. I prayed hard. Not to anyone in particular, because God and I had not made up yet, but I asked for help from up above that I still be given the chance to walk out of here on my healed feet, to start my band and new life.

I woke up to a sight I had not seen since I was seven years old.

My mother and father were in the same room, watching over me without arguing. It takes great adversity at times to silence an ego, and both of them knew that this was a serious matter, and all drama was left at the door.

I was prepped for surgery and given the pill that was to calm me before the onslaught of grafting was to take place all over my body.

Within minutes I had my eyes closed and the last thing I heard were the soft voices of both my mother and father talking about me and supporting me by being there together in peace.

I felt like a child of five again with my mommy and daddy tucking me in after reading me a story. I hadn't heard those voices together in that way for 16 years, and I have never heard them that way since. At that moment, life was bliss as I drifted off into the deep abyss.

Waking up from this surgery, I did not feel like death warmed over, but I definitely felt a new level of pain.

My thighs were literally on fire, where they peeled the good skin off, and placed it on my wounds that were shaved with something that resembles a cheese grater in order for the good skin to at some point attach to the grated wounds.

Words cannot describe the pain adequately. My whole body was on fire with pain, yet I was so excited to be alive again.

The days and nights that followed in the Grossman Burn Ward were pretty uneventful. Meals were brought in, and nurses checked my levels. Each friend who visited for the first time had a look of horror on their face when they saw me. My skin literally looked like Freddy Kruger on my arms, hands, legs, feet and now thighs.

Their look of horror was met by my smile and laughter at being alive to see a person I loved.

They did not understand how someone who was in so much pain could be so happy, and my answer was, "I am still here to see you. I am happy to be breathing."

Dr. Grossman was telling me that I may not be able to walk the same again. He warned me that I definitely would not be able to go back to my former employment as a retail manager because of all of the hours of standing I had to do in that job.

He wasn't even sure that he could save one of my toes, and he also warned that the burning was so deep on my hands and fingers, that I may not have any feeling in them ever again.

I heard the words, but that same deep inner wisdom that knew I would someday start my own band, knew that I would definitely walk again, keep all 10 toes and have feeling in my hands again.

Truth be told, I hated being a retail manager for JoAnn's Fabrics and Crafts, so that part I took in, and told myself that once I was out of the burn ward, I would find a job that had more structure. I hadn't had two days off in a row for years, because the manager always has to be in the store to keep things going, especially during the holidays and through payroll cuts.

Since I was a manager, and made the schedule, I always put myself to close, so I didn't have to arrive at work until 1pm. That gave me plenty of time to sleep in after the non-stop party that I lived in.

I worked hard, and was very responsible when I was at work, but because I was so scattered in life and where I lived, I never really figured out the balance between quiet time and party time. It was hard to find quiet time where I lived, and since I was in my early 20s, I never really felt I needed it.

The new me was excited for the change, and had grown to like quiet time; being away from the party houses of my past. I took to meditation in the Grossman Burn Ward, because there wasn't much else to do, and I was concentrating on manifesting the perfect job once I was all healed up.

The Universe answered me back about the job in the form of my friend Sabino's friend, Trish.

Trish was a loud and boisterous woman who reminded me of Janis Joplin in looks, energy, voice and definitely laugh. She had the same look of horror that everyone did upon the first time viewing my skin, but quickly laughed with me, as I told the story of what happened, and explained really how lucky I was to be alive.

Her first words to me were, "You have such an amazing outlook on life. Are you in sales?" When I answered, "I was a Retail Manager, but I can't do that anymore. I can't be on my feet that long."

She told me not to worry, that she worked at a TV rep firm in the advertising industry, and that when I was healed up and ready to work to call her, and she would get me in as an assistant.

My wish answered. A Monday-Friday 9-5pm job with evenings off, weekends off, holidays off, medical benefits and 401K! I couldn't wait for the life change from days of sleeping, afternoons of being a retail manager and nights of boozing it up.

Now even more than just wanting to start the band, I couldn't wait to get out to start my new life! New home, new car, new job and new band! I had so much living to do, now I just needed the skin grafts to take, so I could fly into my renewed purposes in life!

This extreme high was the prelude to the biggest Dark Night of The Soul that I have ever experienced closing in on me.

YOUR HEALING ACTION!

Please log onto www.thehealingwoods.com/book-bonus/ in order to access your next bonus to further your own personal journey of igniting your light within!

CHAPTER 3

DARK NIGHT OF THE SOUL

In order for the light to shine so brightly, the darkness must be present.

—Francis Bacon

Dr. Grossman came in to look at how my progress was going after the autografting, and as he unwrapped the bandages, my heart sank as the same gory patchwork of nightmares stared back at me. It did not appear to be any better than it was a week ago, and the pain was still the same as having hot irons constantly sitting on 30% of my body.

He shook his head, and told me that if these grafts did not take soon, I would have to get another round of grafting, which meant another donor site, and even more areas of pain on my already tortured skin.

My spirit died when I heard that. I shut down, and the smiling happy-to-be-alive girl darkened into a depressed lump of burned flesh who had no hope left.

In my darkened hospital room, I wondered why, if there was a God, why He put me through losing my car to a semi-truck on Friday, burning myself and my house down on Saturday and stopping my heart on the operating table a few days later?

What Karma was I releasing? I must have been Hitler in a past life to deserve all of this.

Now I was being told that I could be in here for months until the grafting takes, and if we didn't start seeing improvement on the soles of the feet, I would lose the toe and could have issues walking again.

The part of me that fought hearing that the first time he said it gave in, and resignation took over where determination once stood.

I also did not have any visitors that day to cheer me up, and the only phone call I received was from the wife of the landlord who owned the house I burned down.

She had me on the phone for half an hour, asking if I was OK, and telling me not to worry about the house, that they had insurance. She also said she was praying for me, and asked if she could pray with me on the phone.

Her prayer went something like this, "Please Lord God, forgive Kristin, and all of the darkness she has suffered through. Show her your light and take her into your forgiving arms. She knows not what she has done, and is still your child, even though on a truly dark path."

She asked me if I believed in God, and I said, "No. I believe in Nature, but right now I am finding it hard to believe in anything."

She went on and on about God taking away my sins, and the fire being something I deserved to burn away all of the times I ignored him. This lady was a real piece of work, and obviously one of the Born Again Christians gone wrong.

I hung up the phone feeling even worse about myself and life than I ever had. I questioned why I was even brought back, and if it was just for more torture and pain.

I cried for over an hour on the phone to one of my best friends, Jamie, who let us stay at her house the night after the fire.

She was one of the only true witchy friends I met since my meeting of Mary, my first witch ever. Jamie was a bit older than I was, and successful and happy in life, so she was just the right kind of light I desperately needed within that deep dark well of emotion I was drowning in.

I cried to Jamie about the landlord's wife telling me I was evil and that it was God's way of punishing me. I told her that I was a bad person, and how much pain I was in. I was really feeling the victim role intensely, and not able to see any of the light I exuded in the prior weeks.

Jamie listened to my weeping fears, and lovingly told me to snap out of it.

She told me the landlord's wife was insane, and that she knew me well, and that I was definitely the opposite of a bad person. She was real with me, and said that she saw right through my antics in life, and knew that I was in huge amounts of anger and pain, but evil, I definitely was not.

Jamie saved my life that night, and after being "talked down out of my tree" as she says, I hung up the phone exhausted. I looked up at the hospital ceiling in the dark room lit only by medical device displays. I spoke to The Goddess, God, The Universe, anyone who would listen.

I prayed again, and I prayed hard.

I asked for help. I needed something to help me heal. I didn't want to have to go through another skin graft surgery. I wanted my skin to heal on its own, and I needed to keep all my toes, be able to walk normally and have feeling in my hands again.

I wanted to be able to sing again, and write; to laugh and love.

I was tired of my whole existence being loss and pain. I had a month of it, and I learned my lesson well. I told whoever was listening up there, "I know I received this lesson because I am strong enough to take it, but I am only human, and I am about to break. Please send help. Send it now!"

At that moment, I felt a huge rush in my head, and sensed a very warm energetic presence enter the room. I felt myself getting very dizzy, and an energetic suctioning on all of my burns and donor sites began.

I started to feel myself being lifted out of my body, and I immediately got scared. I told whoever was listening up there, "I don't want to die…please don't take me!"

That inner wisdom that I had lost took over again, and I was assured that whatever was happening was for my soul's greatest good, and I should allow it to continue.

I let go, and felt myself rise completely out of my body and up towards the ceiling.

For the first time in a month, I felt no pain whatsoever, and it felt amazing! I had forgotten what it was to live pain-free; it had been so long.

All time stood still, and all thoughts disappeared. I felt as though I was in the womb of The Universe and being given the most beautiful Divine energetic hug. All was right in the world, and I felt as if I had come home.

I could have been up there five minutes or five days. I had no concept of time at all, but when I felt myself being lowered back down to my body. There was a part of me that feared what was waiting for me back on earth in that body, but that same inner wisdom told me to trust, and all will be OK.

I felt myself hit my body, and I came to. I moved my limbs around, and I was in shock that someone had turned off the hot irons that had been attached to my skin for a month!

I still had the gory nightmarish quilt skin, and I could feel the tightness of the skin grafts and donor sites as I moved, but only about 10-percent of the pain and heat remained.

I had the sudden urge to urinate, and decided it's now or never, let's test this out when I walk on my burnt feet to the bathroom.

For the couple weeks prior, I was healed enough on the bottoms of my feet to slowly hobble five feet to the bathroom, but it took me about five minutes to actually get out of bed, and another few minutes to slowly drag myself near the toilet. Then, it took me holding my breath and slowly bending my donor site thighs to actually sit on the toilet.

All of this brought on huge grimaces of pain, which I was used to seeing when I walked past the hospital bathroom mirror.

This time, I prepared for the pain of getting out of bed, but no pain met me. I easily got out of bed, and took my first step, with no outburst of groaning like the past couple weeks brought out of me.

I walked into the same bathroom that for weeks I hobbled into and looked at my face in that same mirror that I would catch glimpses of pain in daily.

When you are in the burn ward, there are no showers. The only type of bathing you do is a water torture device they call Whirlpool, because burns cannot have hard water hit them. Every other day I was wheeled into the Whirlpool room, and my bandages were taken off, which was extremely painful, and I was set in the Whirlpool, which was a large metal tub, with soft water constantly flowing around me.

The nurses would have to clean my wounds, and as I wrote in my burn journal about the experience, "Every time I go into Whirlpool, I am in so much pain and crying so hard that I actually want my mommy."

Whirlpool does not wash your hair, so it had been weeks since my hair was washed. My hair was oily and sweaty in a ratty ponytail, my face was puffy from tears and I was in a drab hospital gown. Not photo ready, by any means.

When I looked at my face in that same mirror that showed me my pain day after day, I caught a glimpse of my eyes, and I saw the fire burning within them. They were alive and beautiful and for the first time in 23 years of life, I actually felt love for the person who looked back at me in that mirror.

For 15 years, I struggled with who I was, and being able to love her or even just not hate her.

My life was not the worst ever recorded up to that point, but I had definitely been through some drama. I took all of it in, and had problems releasing it in a constructive way. As a result, there was a lot of anger lying beneath the surface, and the anger was usually focused on myself, and how unworthy and unlovable I was.

For the first time ever that night in the harsh lighting of the bathroom, I loved me. I looked in that mirror and saw beauty. I saw power. I saw love.

I was beautiful powerful love, and the emotions overcame me.

I spent the next 3 hours sitting on my hospital bed trying my best to scribble in my burn journal about this experience.

Here are some of those pieces of the first love letter I had ever written myself:

I just had an amazing out of body experience. It is 1:25am, and I am so excited by what I just experienced, that I had to get up and try my hardest to write in my fire journal even though my hands are all bandaged up and almost useless.

I was lying in my hospital bed, and all of a sudden I felt very fevered, drunk and like I was about to faint. It felt as if my body was being pulled to one side of the room, and I sensed a warm energy come into the room.

I'm going to test this theory out in a moment, but I believe that something just came into my hospital room and suctioned the pain out of me because I can move around more freely in my bed and where my wounds are feels very warm and light.

I have to pee, so I will be right back to report how the pain is....

I don't know what or who just helped me, but I seriously felt no pain!

I felt the wounds stretch and they are still red and inflamed, but the usual throbbing and pain are all but gone!

I am far from completely healed, but I am so in shock that my pain is gone! Funny how earlier today, I was crying and asking for anyone listening in the spirit realm to help me with my pain. I was heard.

This last trip to the bathroom was the quickest and least painful I've had since these fucking burns plagued me. I am so happy to know that I have turned a corner, and I can finally feel some relief from the constant pain I have been enduring.

A month straight of pain…I've never felt so much in my whole life put together. Maybe the fire happened because for so long I had been so dead inside. Now every nerve in my body is used to being awake to feel every bit of pain my wounds have to offer.

The way I look now horrifies me. I have wounds like Freddie Kruger on my arms, hands, legs and feet, my hair hasn't been washed in weeks and I have been in a very unflattering hospital gown for my whole stay here.

On my way to the toilet a few minutes ago, I caught a glimpse of myself, and yes…even though my hair was a mess and in a tangled pony tail…my eyes are alive, vibrant and on fire! I look refreshed and ready to take on the world, when usually, as I glanced in that same mirror, I'd see my face scrunched up in a pain-filled grimace and my eyes dull and lifeless except to express the pain I was in.

I believe I am waking up.

I believe it is now my turn to finally live life.

I know I have survived.

I know I can do anything I put my clear mind to…and I will…I can…I AM!

When I started writing this entry 40 minutes ago, I had no idea it would turn into a love letter to myself, but it is wonderful that it has. This is the first love letter I have ever even thought to write to me.

The last 5 years have usually given birth to endless journal entries written in the wee hours of the morning about lost love, no love and self hate.

I now know myself too well to hate her, and although there are things I want to change about her outsides…inside she is tough, she is loving, she is good, kind, caring and what right do I have to hate her? NONE!!!

I'm still alive and damn it, if I do only one thing in my re-given life, it is going to be to learn to completely love me.

This is the first night in my whole life that I have felt love for me. Even when I was in a relationship with someone I didn't feel love for myself, so this whole "I need to find a mate to make me whole" shit is finally over.

I need myself to make me whole and I am the only person who can find out who she is now, because she has changed. Her whole history as far as material possessions is gone but there's a lot of heart and soul history alive between us that

I will never forget…how could I ever hate that?

She has had enough people kick her and put her down in her 23 years of life…why should I be one more?

She needs to stand tall, and be who she is because she is me and we finally love each other tonight!

I am going to live my life to get used to that love. I love me.

I woke up the next morning to a pain free trip to Whirlpool, and the deepest feeling of peace I could remember since childhood.

A couple days later, Dr. Grossman came to see how my progress was going, and I couldn't wait to tell him my pain had all but vanished!

He looked at me a bit confused, because just a few days prior, we were having the conversation about the extreme possibility of needing to do more skin grafting.

He opened up my bandages, and a smile came over his face as he exclaimed, "Wow, your grafting really has taken a turn for the better, and these are really looking great! If this healing continues, you will be out of here by the end of the week!"

I was so elated that I looked up towards the hospital room ceiling, into the invisible portal where I knew that Divine Energy came from and mouthed, "Thank you." It's a practice I still do to this day as a token of gratitude for something that goes beautifully in my life.

The healing continued quickly, and I was released from the womb of the Grossman Burn Ward into the healing household of my beautiful mother, who took me in, and gave me a safe place to strengthen up.

After living with tons of people in party houses from age 17 to 23, I was ready to finally live by myself. I prepared for my new, stable 9-5 job in Corporate America; it was just the thing that allowed the home of my own to manifest.

YOUR
HEALING ACTION!

Please log onto
www.thehealingwoods.com/book-bonus/
in order to access your next bonus to further your own personal journey of igniting your light within!

CHAPTER 4

LIFE OUT OF THE BURNT COCOON

The most beautiful stories always start with wreckage.

—Jack London

Although the fire woke me from a slumber of drug use, depression and stagnation, it took me some time to be able to physically do the things my spirit knew I needed to accomplish.

I was far from completely healed when I was released. I still had nurses visiting me at home to do wound care and I was not able to really walk further than to the next room for another month.

Through it all, I was so excited for the new life which was coming, and I felt a huge excitement for the next phase of growth, which would be moving out of my mom's house once I was healed and working again, and into a place without any roommates.

I remember how light it felt to have literally all of my belongings fit into one hefty trash bag.

I spent most days resting in between visits from the in-home nurses, wound care and visits from friends.

When I was able to actually put on some sandals and walk around for a bit, some friends came to pick me up and we went out to see a movie. I can't for the life of me tell you what movie it was, but I can still to this day remember how amazing it felt to laugh out loud with my friends, eat horrible nachos and have the ability to walk to the car after.

To not be tied to a Morphine drip for the first time in a month, to wear shoes without huge white bandages covering my healing feet and to lose myself in a stupid movie amongst the living was the medicine my soul needed.

The healing process of burns was a slow but steady one. Once the open wounds were securely grafted and new skin took over, it was exactly that…brand new thin skin much like a baby would have.

My hands were so alive with feeling, that I swear I could feel dust particles in the air. I was told my Dr. Grossman that was normal for the new baby skin to be extremely sensitive. I felt textures so intensely, and temperature changes were incredible. If I had my hands in cold water, I had to warm them up before picking up a hot cup of coffee, or else the heat from the coffee would be too much all at once.

When I rubbed soap onto my body during showers, I could feel every single fine hair on the landscape of my skin.

To this day, whenever I get a pedicure, I am so intensely ticklish on my feet, which never happened before the fire.

Learning to cope with this new skin was interesting, and I always felt as if I literally was a newborn baby who was experiencing the world again for the first time as a totally different person post-fire.

Emotionally, I was going through some issues within this rebirth as well. It was the first time in six years that I was back living with my mom after being on my own. I moved out the day after high school graduation for a reason, and within my six years of living like a free gypsy moving from camp to camp, the reason became fuzzy.

Moving back in, the reasons became crystal clear. We do not do well living together, and our relationship is much better when we each have our own worlds to retreat back into.

Today I can look back in complete and utter gratitude that she was there to take me in when I could not walk, and gave me a place to heal rent free, but it was not completely free to be there. A lot of tears, arguing and drama made up the price of my brief time living back home.

Our relationship was bad enough when I was a teenager struggling for freedom, and sneaking out of my bedroom window every chance I got to go to a goth club, acid party or just to drive around Hollywood Blvd with my gay boyfriend, Sabino.

In high school, I really had no idea what freedom actually was, and was made to grasp for it any chance I got within the cloak of night after my mom fell asleep.

Once I moved out, I had six years of nothing but freedom. Going to clubs four nights a week, staying out all night if I wanted, heading off on a roadtrip to wherever, whenever with whoever I wanted and through all of this, keeping a steady job and paying my rent on time.

I was the perfect alchemical balance of fuck up and responsible young adult.

It was extremely hard to go right back into the restrictive home of my mother after being that free, and adding to the mix not really being able to walk and not feeling comfortable doing much of anything there except popping Vicodin and sleeping.

The pain was still throbbing, but I do admit that I could have handled it without the drugs. However, I ended up self-medicating the emotional turmoil I was going through living with my mom again and us fighting like cats and dogs through my healing.

There were many times we had screaming matches, and I packed my hefty trash bag full of my sparse belongings with the intention of leaving, but then realized I had no car thanks to the semi-truck accident and I had no job or money, so I popped another pill to ease the harsh reality of how stuck I was in life.

Today I love my mom more than words can describe.

She taught me how to be a strong independent woman, how to do things on my own and always had my back whenever an emergency came up, which was many times on my crazy E Ticket ride called life.

In the months coming out of the fire in 1998, I did not have the wisdom to see where our relationship would grow to once I was allowed to be free and grow into the woman I am today.

In 1998, I was stuck in a seemingly neverending loop of aggression between the two of us, and I realized that I needed to get my feet back on the ground (literally), and be able to walk on them. I had to buy a car using the settlement money from the semi-truck accident and find another job.

Slowly but surely all of these things came to pass. I had my new/used car, I was able to walk on my own and drive myself around and I was finally ready to test out my wobbly new wings as a phoenix.

My healing exploded with my determination to obtain personal freedom once again, and I was able to walk perfectly, kept all of my toes and had feeling in my hands.

I was strong and ready to work, but I was definitely still learning how to cope with the aftermath of major skin graft surgery and third-degree burns.

Trish completely followed through with getting me an interview at the TV rep firm she worked at called Blair Television in Santa Monica, California.

With everything I owned in the world fitting into one large trash bag, I did not have any outfits to wear to an interview. After all, the past couple months I spent either in a hospital gown or PJ's.

I only had two outfits that I was able to buy with the $100 clothes voucher from The Red Cross I received the day of the fire, and neither of them were suitable for an interview at a swanky advertising firm in West LA. I bought my first corporate America interview outfit with the help of my mother, and showed up to my first of many high-rises on the Westside.

The interview was very long and tedious and involved many people that kept coming in and out of the huge glass fishbowl conference room overlooking the Pacific Ocean.

I was used to just jumping from store to store, and people calling me to clean up their store. In the retail manager world, I was a big fish.

In the turbulent sea of the advertising world, I was mere plankton.

Even though I was plankton, I knew I was the toughest breed of plankton. Plus, I was grounded and centered within my power, and had an answer for every single question they threw at me.

What I lacked in a college education, I more than delivered with the life experience and management experience I had at age 23. No college graduate looking for an entry level assistant job was a living breathing phoenix, and I owned that and exuded that.

I knew others felt that too; as person after person came in scowling at me, and left smiling.

One even asked for a hug.

Days later, I was hired, and I started my first day of 12 years of an hour-and-a-half commute each way to get from the beautiful mountains of Altadena, California to the concrete jungle of West Los Angeles to climb the corporate ladder of the advertising world.

At this point in life, I had tattoos, a nose ring and multicolored hair, and somehow still got into the suit-and-tie vanilla world of the advertising world. I wasn't dealing with clients as an assistant, so I was able to fit in as best as I could by covering the tattoos, wearing stylish-yet-office-acceptable dark clothing, and shining as brightly as I could by doing a good job and having an amazing attitude even though most of the people around me were neurotic, alcoholic stressed out messes.

Most of the women I encountered my first years as an assistant were a breed of angry "media bitch" with a propensity towards alcoholism. I was really thrown to the sharks at Blair TV. When I told Trish which Account Executive I would be assisting, she said, "Oh wow. She's tough. You'll be OK though."

Being a manager at fabric and craft stores was a woman's world, but now I was in a Boy's Club, and most of the women Advertising Executives (AE's) had to be tough in order to succeed in that testosterone driven club.

I moved out on my own the day after I graduated from high school, and began working full time to pay my bills. I never finished college, nor did I obtain a degree.

All of the assistants I sat next to on the sales floor were all about my same age, early 20s, and all had degrees in business and marketing. The male assistants were strutting around like peacocks, and the women were watching closely as the Female AE's showed them the ins and outs of being a Media Bitch. I had the Queen of all Media Bitches as a direct boss.

The fact that I was able to afford to move out on my own to a tiny cabin up in the foothills surrounded by trees made all of the struggle, stress and tears I cried driving to and from work worth it.

People always asked me why I commuted so far, and why was I not looking for a place closer to work? I just smiled and said, "I can't leave the foothills for the city. Those mountains have my soul."

Of course most people in the advertising world had no idea what I was talking about and just smiled and nodded as they went about their media lives, but I knew that I still had a lot of healing to do inside. Now that the outer burns had healed, being in the womb of Nature that is Altadena, CA was where I had my sights set.

I had no desire whatsoever to move into the concrete jungle just to be closer to the Boy's Club. In fact, I loved being far away from it on the weekends, because I felt release from it. I was able to enjoy my time off, not having to see the high-rise I worked in looming in the distance as I am trying to go about my day was worth the drive.

I was living with my mom in Arcadia when I first started working at Blair. I had my sights set on Altadena, because it was very close to the mountains, and I felt like I needed their grounding and healing through this process of figuring out exactly who I was after the fire claimed me as its own.

I was not making a lot of money as an assistant, perhaps $20,000 a year, but it was enough for a small place, and I knew I needed to live alone even though it scared me to death.

Since moving out on my own at age 17, I had been in communal living situations with anywhere from three to ten other people living in the house, and I knew that I had learned all of the lessons I could about myself within community, and that now it was time for me to do it on my own.

It scared me because I didn't yet know who I was, and a lot of who I thought I was revolved around my tribe of people I always had close to me. I never had to look far for a group of people to accompany me to a bar, club, random road trip or drug trip, and living alone meant I would have to figure out who and what I was…alone.

It scared me financially as well. I was able to skate by paying $300 rent for one bedroom in a four-bedroom place with ten people splitting rent, but paying all the rent alone, plus the utilities, would be difficult.

I knew I absolutely could not live in an apartment. I did that twice, and really hated it. I needed to be on the ground, near nature and not in a huge complex upstairs with strangers living on all sides of me.

I knew what I wanted because I had experienced it before. I decided one Full Moon to get real with this list of desires for my new home, and even though it really scared me to say it, I let The Universe know that I was ready willing and able to live completely on my own.

I was meditating on the same lounge chairs of my childhood with a crystal on my third eye, staring up at the full moon. A clear vision of my friend Amber came into my head. I was meditating to gain clarity on my upcoming move, and I thought it was strange that she came to mind for that, since I was not looking for a roommate.

The inner wisdom voice kicked in, and I was on the phone to her, asking her if her landlord had any openings in her courtyard. She didn't live in Altadena in the hills, like I wanted to, but she had a cute little house in a courtyard a few miles from the hills in Pasadena, and I had to start somewhere.

She gave me her landlord's number, and the moment I called, I knew there was a reason I saw Amber in my vision.

Sue was the landlord, and she said that just that day, she had someone in a tiny one bedroom cottage in a courtyard in Altadena give notice, and that it wasn't even out in the papers yet.

The price was perfect, and it was extremely tiny, but I only had about three trash bags full of belongings at this point, besides a bed, so I didn't need much space at all.

I knew the house was mine the moment I set foot in it, and for the first time ever in my life, I made the decision alone on moving into a house.

I moved all of my stuff in one car ride, and nested in my new healing womb that would prove to see many incarnations of me evolve for the next 13 years. Even though at the time, I thought I would just be there for a year to get grounded after the fire.

My healing womb of a home surrounded by trees, with the mountains as a constant backdrop was just perfect for one person.

A mountain lion was kicking it in a tree on my street, the day I moved in, with news vans everywhere trying to catch a glimpse. Squirrels, skunks, raccoons and coyotes were constant companions of my yard. I was in heaven, and getting used to living alone for the first time in my life.

I did have some Post Traumatic Stress Disorder I was dealing with after the fire, and this little healing space gave me the peace in which I needed to work through that. I would wake up screaming from dreams of my house on fire. I would walk into a room and immediately imagine how it would look all burned up. I also would feel a pit of panic in my stomach if I smelled a fireplace burning in the neighborhood.

I went to counseling and got my confidence back with fire slowly but surely with burning incense and candles while being in the same room watching them.

Once I was ready to bring them back in my life as a magical tool, I began using green candles to focus on abundance throughout my career in The Boy's Club.

I was at Blair TV for two years, and during that two years, I moved from assisting the Queen Media Bitch's desk, to assisting the Paid Programming desk (and selling some commercial airtime while assisting the AE), to finally becoming the Team Coordinator who assisted the Sales Manager of the whole team.

I worked long hours, and some weekends making sure everything got done, but I always had a smile on my face for anyone, especially the assistants, who came to my office for help.

The longer I was there, and the more I let out parts of who I was, the more I noticed people coming out of the woodwork to connect with me about their spiritual questions. It got out that I read tarot and meditated, so I would have women coming to see me all the time to have deep spiritual talks in the middle of a world that celebrates plastic and commerce.

Soul-deep conversations within the stress and excess of the media industry became the norm for me. It would happen within my office at work, and even at the huge industry parties around town, and conventions in Vegas. I never ever lost sight of who I was through it all, and for that I am ever so grateful.

Later in my career as a manager, I was expected to forge relationships with buyers and TV station managers, and I was always the one who was able to create a good relationship with the toughest and most unruly people in the business. I believe that is because the higher up on the ladder I went, the more of who I was showed.

Towards the end of my career in the advertising world, I was also the lead singer of a goth band, and promoted my shows to my colleagues. It always made me giggle when I saw a group of media people in business casual attire standing out in the sea of black wearing goths staring up at the stage I was performing on.

Perhaps they knew just a little bit, standing in that club, how it felt being me in their world when I first began.

I won the toughest people in the industry over because I stood out from the norm and I was fiercely me. My dry sense of humor, my calming tone and my amazing work ethic blew their defenses out of the water. At times I even had some of the toughest men break down after a few martinis at a media function, and tell me some heavy secrets and ask my advice on life.

It was just who I was; the secret keeper and spiritual wisdom giver to the starving souls within the ad industry.

In order to become the woman who would one day create her own position as Regional Sales Manager for Paid Programming, the girl who was stuck at the glass ceiling of being a Team Coordinator at Blair TV realized she needed to leave the company in order to move up.

I was looking online at job postings, and saw one at Fox TV Sales for an Administrative Manager. This would be a huge upgrade from where I currently was at Blair. It meant that I would be assisting the VP Director of Sales of the whole office, and I would be in charge of all assistants on the sales floor as well as dealing with ordering supplies, doing payroll and all Human Resources for the entire office.

It scared the shit out of me to apply, and I almost didn't, but the inner wisdom voice spoke again, and I found myself pressing send on the e-mail to the VP of Fox with my pulse racing and my stomach churning.

After a less grueling interview with only one person, I was hired, and showed where my office was. I had my first office door, which was a huge thing in the ridiculous hierarchy of office politics.

The day my nameplate was slid onto the door, I felt a huge rush of pride that the Goth chick with tattoos and a nose ring is now sitting in this lofty office with a view of a beautiful tree lined courtyard, as the Administrative Manager of Fox TV Sales.

I didn't have a college degree like many of the The Boy's Club who went for the same position I just landed, but I had tons of real work experience, did many years of payroll at the stores I managed and worked my way up the corporate ladder at Blair Television.

Plus, The Boy's Club hadn't ever stared death directly in the face and survived like I had.

I immediately soared on my new bigger and stronger phoenix wings, and created a whole new system for that office to receive half hour and hour long commercials called Paid Programming from the New York Office. No one in that office had ever dealt with Paid Programming, but I was on the Paid Programming desk before becoming a supervisor at Blair, so I used all of that systems knowledge to build the team at Fox.

I still had to deal with some craziness at Fox, because the VP made my first Queen of Media Bitches look like a little kitten, but at this point I was a Fire Warrior, and nothing a Media Bitch could throw at me would break my stride.

I had pictures of redwoods, ocean and desert scenes littering the walls around my desk where most other people had TV stars and sports figures. I had crystals within close reach, tons of thriving plants and a fountain running at all times.

People all around me in the lifeless grey office were bursting into tears; running down the hall to get to the bathroom to weep; slamming doors and managers were yelling about budgets in the background. Somehow I kept my cool through it all.

I would have assistants coming into my office crying about how stressed out they were. I would even have Account Executives come in to get away from the madness of their desks.

I actually had one high level manger come in, take a deep breath and say, "I feel like I'm going to the spa every time I visit you. I feel so much more calm near you."

I attribute my ability to keep calm through over a decade within this Media Hell to my attunements to Reiki.

The moment I started working, and collecting paychecks from The Boy's Club at Blair TV, I started to seek out that Divine energy I felt within the Grossman Burn Ward to see where on Earth I could experience it again.

I went to angel healers, crystal healers, shamans and all sorts of different energy workers searching out that Divine energy. Finally when I had my first Reiki session, I felt that same warmth and lightness that I felt in the burn ward. Not as strongly, because it wasn't the Universe doing the healing directly, but it was very similar, and I knew that my soul's path was set to travel through the journey of becoming a Reiki Master.

Reiki has three levels, and the first level of attunements is meant for clearing you out and empowering you to be able to focus on self-healing through Reiki.

Some Reiki Masters teach Reiki 1 and 2 together, but I am a big believer that doing them together is a great disservice to the beauty and power that Reiki 1 provides for people.

We must heal ourselves before we can help facilitate in anyone else's healing. When I received my Reiki 1 attunements, I went on a journey with Reiki 1 for many years before even thinking about moving up to the next level to be able to work on others.

The day of my Reiki 1 attunement changed my life, but the change was slow but deep…not noticeable the day of, but years later, I was a completely and utterly different person.

Before Reiki, I doubted myself and allowed myself to be tied to people, places and things that kept me tethered to a way of life that I knew, instead of allowing myself to fly up to the level I deserved to be at.

I attribute me finally being able to be seen on stage as the lead singer of a band to the clearing I did within Reiki.

I loved singing, and did it well.

I was even paid to sing certain songs at Karaoke dive bars and told I should start a band, but my fear of owning that power and gift and really showing it on a soul level scared the crap out of me. So onto the next Karaoke Bar I went to sing White Rabbit time and time again just to get the release of singing and feel the energy of the audience, such as they were at the dive bars.

Once I was attuned to Reiki and went on the long journey of self-healing, I felt as if multiple layers of sadness and fear were peeled off of me, and I was allowed a glimpse into just how much more healing I had to do on myself in order to break free from my binds of past pain.

I felt lighter and freer. I felt reborn once again, and strong with a new weapon of self-healing that showed itself to me on my darkest night of the soul in the Grossman Burn Clinic.

Reiki showed me who I really was, and what I had to break out of in order to be who I came back here a second time to be.

Reiki showed me who the people around me were underneath their masks, which caused me to grow further apart from the toxic people in my life, while making room for new teachers and partners in healing.

I felt empowered to dive deeply into my inner sadness and rage. The level that never shows itself in your day to day life, but can flow into your thoughts when you are alone, and slow down enough to allow its rumblings into your heart.

I did some amazing work on myself within these years of being at Reiki Level 1, and am glad I spent that time on me to clear myself out as much as I could and master level 1 before moving onto helping others within Reiki level 2.

My Reiki level 2 attunement brought an amazing level of peace to me. It showed me the deep well of strength I have, and also helped me guard myself from other people's emotions and energies, so I could be the strongest conduit of Reiki energy I could be for the people I was practicing on.

The beauty of helping others with Reiki is that I am not putting my energy into them, or taking out any of their energy into me, rather I am using Universal Life Force energy, which is pure and limitless. I am a conduit of this energy, and it heals me as I help to facilitate in the healing of others.

To this day, after all of the healing miracles I have seen Reiki accomplish on myself as well as on my clients, I am still the first to say that it is the Reiki healing them, not me. I am just a clear channel for the energy to flood through into them, which helps their body's systems function to their fullest potential.

Reiki really is like a muscle. The more you use it, the stronger it gets. Since I was obsessed with using Reiki from the moment I was attuned, I created ways with which I could live Reiki instead of just do Reiki, and my Reiki therefore became stronger and stronger.

At this point, it was just for my own development and healing, not to start a new career at all. I was so busy with the immense piles of paperwork all around me, that I couldn't even think about anything but work for quite some time.

Even with the tools of healing around and within me, I was feeling the burn of stress, and I came to the conclusion that I needed a new release. I needed to do something creative.

I needed music and singing to come back into my life in a deep way.

I needed to manifest being the lead singer of a band.

YOUR
HEALING ACTION!
Please log onto
www.thehealingwoods.com/book-bonus/
in order to access your next bonus to further
your own personal journey of igniting
your light within!

CHAPTER 5

BECOMING DEMONIKA DARKLY

Those who wish to sing always find a song.

— Swedish Proverb

In my Freshman year of high school, I had a Gothic nickname that I used with my best friend at the time, Christel. She was Lilith, and I was Demonika. We would write each other notes using these names, and sometimes I would even use that name when introducing myself at various Goth clubs that I ventured into.

With the armor of the Gothic style of black veils, black clothes, black capes, black lipstick and black nails, I kept people away in high school that I thought would hurt me. I kept them away with intimidation, and felt so totally alone in my darkness.

I had a very small number of friends who enjoyed the same music I did, but even they didn't really understand who I was, and this was partly because I didn't even understand who I was.

I was half-nerd, half-freak; half-honors student, half-ditcher almost failing towards the end of my senior year. I was half-loner, half-tarot reader for all groups of students when I decided to bring my cards out.

I was a living breathing dichotomy.

Music really was my happy place, even though most of the songs I listened to were funeral dirges made from sad minor chords and wailing lyrics of pain, destitute and anger. I suppose it made me happy to know that I wasn't the only one in this whole wide world in pain. Singing along to other people's pain gave me relief and solace.

I was one of three Goths in my high school. The three of us mixed in quite well with the punks, skaters and "art fags" as the more popular people called the creatives. All of us misfits stuck together within our weirdness, but even within the gathering of misfits in Monrovia High School, I still felt utterly alone.

I would be excited about a new Bauhaus song I found in the used tape section or the bootleg Cure record album I found, and people tried to be happy for me, but really had no idea what these bands meant to me.

It wasn't until going to my first Cure concert did I realize that there were more than 3 of us Goths out there; in fact, there was a whole Dodger Stadium filled with us, present for the 1988 Prayer Tour.

I remember staring out into the sea of my black clothes, white face-makeup, spider web eye makeup wearing brethren and for the first time in my pre-teen/adolescent life, I felt safe and at home.

The musical lineup was amazing for this event. The Cure, Love and Rockets and The Pixies. Three of my favorite bands at the time, and with this being the first concert I'd chosen to go to on my own, I was giddy with excitement and teary-eyed with joy through most of it.

I walked around between bands looking at the amazing outfits of the people flooding the hallways and aisles. The ripped up wedding gowns, top hats and canes with skulls on them and long black dresses with beautiful lace trains gliding through the sticky trash lined ground of Dodger Stadium made my soul happy.

I was 13, and at this point I was making most of my outfits and getting what I could from thrift stores. (This is way before Hot Topic and the like were founded; where our current gothic youth can purchase a full outfit readymade for their clubbing needs.)

I was wearing a black skirt I got from a thrift store, which I cut in a ragged Halloween witch costume-like fashion, purple stockings under ripped up shredded black fishnets and a Cure shirt.

I also had my Wet n Wild black lipstick with dark eyeliner on to finish the look. It was the best I could do at age 13, and I was taking many mental notes at the concert for beautiful outfits to have later on in life. This was research.

I saw my first corset there, my first hearse with Goth band stickers all over it and it was the first time I felt safe being me, walking around a huge crowd of people.

Walking around the school campus, I was always on high alert. Every time I walked anywhere I would have food, insults or dirt thrown at me, and had to have my emotional and energetic armor on basically anytime I was awake.

At this magical Cure concert at Dodger Stadium, I experienced the beauty of walking around fully open to everyone around me, and feeling like I was one of the tribe.

Feeling pride that I wore what I wore and screaming out the lyrics with thousands of other people screaming out those same lyrics.

That night, we were all one. We were living gods and goddesses of the Goth scene, and our tribe was strong; our spirits were soaring and we wore the badges of Goth proudly and darkly.

I remember that night, my voice being completely gone, my throat on fire from screaming songs and all of the rings on my fingers were bent from clapping so hard and intensely all night.

I drifted off to sleep with Cure songs dancing through my head, and smiling ear-to-ear knowing that I had found my tribe for the first time in life, and that I would do whatever it took to find more of me out in the world and enjoy my time within the safe space of expression that community brought with it. I was complete.

I soon ventured out to other places where I could find people like me such as music stores, malls and one of my favorites, Marilyn's Backstreet – an underage Goth club in Pasadena, California.

Marilyn's was created for kids aged 12-20, and one night was top 40 music and the other was Goth, Industrial, Ska and some Punk.

I used to spend the night at friends' houses and we would all get ready in our best black outfits to dance the night away with our tribe sipping on Dr. Peppers and eating candy from the bar.

It really was such a sweet place for Baby Goths to get their feet wet in the club scene before the drug-filled bathrooms and alcoholics of the 21 and over clubs came into their lives.

I met my first boyfriend there, I met my first Drag Queen, I met the first friend I would later go to the funeral of because he shot himself, and learned even more deeply about the Goth music and culture I loved so much.

There were some of the older kids who were close to 21 who

would sit in their cars in the parking lot drinking before they went inside to dance, but I never needed to do that. The music and dancing were my drug, and I felt high on life and blissful every time I walked into those black doors.

Every now and then there would be a local band that would play. I can't remember the names of the bands now, but I do remember the feeling I had watching these 20 something year olds playing their dark hearts out amongst the stage fog and twirling purple and blue lights.

Watching them, I felt something inside of me switch on, and I told myself dancing in a sea of black velvet, that one day it would be me who was up on that stage, and promised the scene that I would give back to it within music and imagined people dancing to what I was performing for them.

Little did I know at the time, that my club name "Demonika" would become a very real name within my life years later, and thousands of people would know me as her, and listen to the lyrics she belted out on stage about men that Kristin loved, but didn't have the guts to let them know how she felt.

Demonika had the guts Kristin didn't. She belted out how she felt directly to these men who sometimes were even in the audience. Demonika was the larger than life mouthpiece for Kristin's true emotions, and the need for me to use Demonika as a stage name was born of that magical fairy in my life at the time named Trish who also got me my first job in the advertising industry.

One bright sunny day, a 25-year-old me was gardening in my yard, and planting seeds of music and love in my garden. I always did magical gardening, and planted seeds infused with the things I wanted to bring into my life. Love, abundance, a promotion at work…and this particular day, I was planting seeds of music and singing.

When the plants started to grow from the magical seeds I planted, so did those things show up into my life that I intended.

Trish drove up in her white Miata unannounced with a girl in the passenger seat that I did not know. She introduced her as Jennifer to me, and said something along the lines of, "You are both Goth and like to go to clubs. You should get to know each other!"

Jennifer and I became fast friends, and started to go to clubs together to dance, and moved onto going to see live performances of local bands. One day as we were enjoying appetizers at The Kelly

Mantle Show, I looked at her and said, "We should start a band!" and she looked back at me, and said, "OK!"

Jennifer played violin, and a synthesizer drum machine. She and I spent a couple hours at her apartment one night doing a cover of Jefferson Airplane's "White Rabbit" and a band was officially born.

I finally took all of those years of practice singing on Karaoke stages and found my own voice with the music being created around me. This was the small beginning of 12 years of growth, power and music, and I will always love the feeling I had that first night at Jennifer's house. It felt like the same excitement and bliss I had showing up at the magical Cure Concert more than a decade before.

We didn't have anything to record with, and wanted to get another instrument in the band, so I told my long time friend Vivian about what we were doing, and she said she had a fourtrack, and would love to hear what we were creating. She came to listen, and a bass player was born in the band.

It came time to think of a name, and since Jennifer and I were still very much in the Goth scene and dancing out at the clubs weekly, I wanted to use the name I created for myself when I first discovered the beauty of Goth and resurrected Demonika Darkly. We thought it would be funny if we all have names that started with D, and as a nod to The Ramones, and we all had the last name Darkly.

I was Demonika Darkly, Jennifer was Devlyn Darkly and Vivian was Dv8 Darkly, and together, we were Demonika and The Darklings.

We were on fire with creating, and within a few months I got us our first small gig at a dive bar, and a few months after that, I got us a much bigger gig at The Knitting Factory in Hollywood, hosted by a local college radio station, 88.9FM KXLU.

I remember driving into work one morning, and hearing the DJ announce that they were looking for local bands to play this show, and immediately I wanted to put us in the running for it, but the voice of reason said, "We barely have a full set, and haven't played in front of more than 20 people."

To which the inner voice of wisdom said, "Do it anyway." And so I did.

It was one of the best shows ever, because I remember performing our songs for an audience filled with not only friends, but also complete strangers who were bobbing their heads up and down and definitely enjoying what we were offering from the stage.

I gladly took on the role of manager, booker and promoter. Jennifer did our technical stuff and recording, while Vivian did our web stuff. We each did what our strong suit in life was. Together, we were an amazing team, and a full unit.

As the years moved on, our abilities as musicians grew. My voice and depth of lyrical expression also grew. The first album was pretty much straight Goth, and I sang about vampires and evil clowns and all things of a darker nature, but by the time our second album was being created, I was singing about conquering my self-loathing, spiritual growth in the redwoods and healing the pain of lost love.

By the end of our 12th year together as a band, within our final recordings and songs written, I was singing about my dad's alcoholism, meeting a living Saint who showed me how to nurture self-love and a song clearing out old anger and resentment around my childhood.

Our growth as humans and a band gave birth to much more depth than vampires and cover songs.

Demonika dressed fabulously and was in your face. She wore leather corsets, dresses with many beautiful layers and long trains custom made by my beautiful friend, Bree. Lots of glittery make-up and outlandish headpieces like a Gothic Vegas show girl.

This was all to hide the fact that Kristin really hated her body still, and was dealing with self-loathing issues. In the hospital that amazing night, I had fallen in love with my spirit, and the essence of who Kristin was, but not the body which encased her essence.

A man working on a documentary about the Goth scene for HBO approached us. He interviewed us in-depth and showed up to all of our shows to film them. It was quite ironic that someone who was struggling with body hatred and self-loathing was the front woman of an up-and-coming band constantly being filmed.

The Universe has an amazing way of opening doorways to paths for us to go down, in order to do the healing we need to and to grow as we should. Even though it can be really frightening, we must trust the open doors and enter them.

We had photo shoots, video, unretouched photos of live shows all over the internet, live footage on YouTube, not to mention being front and center and singing my soul out to audiences hundreds of times.

The body I loathed was up front and center on the World Wide

Web, and I truly feel like that was the first step in the extremely long journey I have gone through towards acceptance of myself where I am at in my process of transformation.

Working through self-loathing in the public eye definitely caused some changes in me, after it caused me to hide behind consumption of too many party favors.

There was a point where the band was taking off, big-time. We were playing venues like Goth Day at Disneyland, up and down the coast of California and opening up for big names in the Goth scene. This did not happen without much effort being put out on my part of meeting with other bands and club promoters, being seen at Goth clubs and supporting the scene and seeing hundreds of other bands.

Supporting the scene easily turned into shots at the bar and long nights of not remembering how I got home the next morning.

I was heading into my 30th year, and I had two full-time jobs within the band and the media industry.

At this time I was the Regional Sales Manager for the Paid Programming Department of HRP, another Television Rep Firm I was hired at after I couldn't take anymore of the crap from my Queen Media Bitch Boss at Fox. At the same time, I was booker, promoter, lead singer and lyricist for Demonika and the Darklings, which really was a full-time night job.

Now, instead of merely dancing and drinking at the Goth clubs I had grown so fond of, I was actually playing in them; bringing into fruition the promise that I made to the Goth scene at age 14 when I was at Marilyn's Backstreet.

In order to get the shows in which to play in the clubs, someone had to be there night after night to support the club, see other bands, friend said bands and promoters and then finally being invited to play a show after sometimes multiple times asking and handing off demos.

It was not easy, but I loved it. It fed my passion, and I was happy to do it, even though it meant I was usually living on three-to-four hours of sleep a night, if I was lucky.

The guy who was doing the documentary on the Goth scene simply loved that I was a high-powered executive manager in the Advertising Industry by day, and the Lead Singer of a Goth Band by night.

I loved it, too.

Even if I was stressed out by my day job, I had an upcoming

show or creating lyrics to be excited about. I was the perfect balance of corporate executive and artistic freak. Much like when I was in high school being the gifted honors student almost failing out of senior year because of ditching.

I would wake up at 7am to fight traffic to barely make it to HRP on the Westside by 9am, and after I got home, I would head out go hit the club scene playing shows or promoting until 2am for the band.

My time was never my own, it was owned by my passion for the band and my need to collect a paycheck from a high-stress sales manager position. After a few years of this, something had to give. And it did, as a big part of my Saturn Return.

In Astrology, a Saturn Return happens every 27-30 years, and it is when Saturn returns to where it was within the sky the day you were born.

Saturn is the planet of huge life lessons, Karma and work. It is usually not a very pleasant time in life, and a Saturn Return can be especially jarring for someone who was as busy and ungrounded as I was, always saying yes to everyone except myself.

Saturn had his way with me one evening, and I received my first and only DUI, as I was leaving a media industry party.

My car was towed; I lost my license; I had to be driven to work for a month, and go to AA meetings and alcohol classes. I also had to pay huge fees to lawyers and the City of Santa Barbara, where I received the DUI.

I ended up having to do four days of community service in Santa Barbara, and had to take time off of work to do so. My boss Joel, the VP of HRP understood about this, and knew that when you are in the "work hard, play hard" media industry, that things like DUI's happen a little too often.

My biggest fear was being put in jail for a month, and I almost was, because I just happened to get this DUI at a time when Santa Barbara was severely cracking down on drunk drivers.

I did not crash into anything or hurt anyone, but I was swerving a bit, as my eyes were off the road trying to read printed out directions in the dark while navigating the car. I hit the line a few times too many, and the red and blue lights appeared like in a bad dream behind me.

They had me get out of the car, and do some field sobriety testing and blow into the breathalyzer machine, which I failed. The next thing I know, I am being handcuffed and thrown into the back of their police car.

I was drunk, but I knew the severity of what was happening, and I was crying and praying to The Universe to help me through this.

My mind went blank as I sat in the back of the police car, and they started driving me to what I believed to be jail for the night when a small miracle happened, and the cop said, "Which hotel are you staying at?"

I told him the name of it, and he said, "Since you cooperated with us so well, and the jail is quite full tonight, we are going to get you back to your hotel instead of taking you in."

Tears of gratitude streamed down my face as I thanked them profusely, and I was driven to the hotel, un-handcuffed and allowed to drag myself up the stairs to my hotel room carrying what seemed like 50 different slips of paper given to me by the cops.

Never will I forget the feeling of dread that washed over me when my alarm went off, and my eyes fluttered open to see the stack of multi-colored papers from the night before. It was as if they were there taunting me and laughing at me that it was not a bad dream, and that this is your life now…deal with it.

I picked up the papers and found out where my car was towed, and called a cab to pick me up to take me to the police station to get the release for my car. The first of hundreds of fines and charges I would have to pay before this whole thing was behind me.

All in all, after the lawyers, fees, classes and car insurance was raised, this DUI ended up costing me somewhere around $14,000, which at the time, might as well have been a million dollars, because I was still in the hole financially from the fire.

I felt as if I had no control whatsoever in life. I was not allowed the freedom to drive; I had tons of meetings and classes I was forced to take, and I was feeling the pull to hermit in my cave and lick my wounds within depression.

The only silver lining to having the DUI be in Santa Barbara was that every time I had to meet with the lawyer, have a court date or do community service, it was in a beautiful seaside city of California which I loved to visit, so I had the arms of Mother Ocean to run to.

Originally, my sentence was going to be a month in jail, but thankfully I had a really great lawyer who was able to get my sentence down to four days of community service.

When I was given the more lenient sentence, I felt like a ton of bricks had been lifted from me, and my stomach was able to untie itself from the hundreds of knots.

When my dates came up to do community service, I booked a hotel room and bought a journal to take with me. My plan was to do the community service then head to the beach, with writing and healing in between.

I was to report to the Santa Barbara County Jail, which was out in the middle of nowhere, but the drive to it was ocean to my left and beautiful mountains to my right, and I spoke to them the whole way there. I listened to their wisdom as well, and they told me that I was to be a prisoner to my vices no more, and the only control I had in my life currently was to control what went into my body.

The drinks; the food; the men. It was time to purge and restrict the only things I still had any control of.

I parked my car in the parking lot, and walked up to the doors to be buzzed in. I was told to leave all of my belongings locked in my trunk and to just bring my photo ID.

I was lead into the jail by two male corrections officers through common areas with male inmates, and it was loud, jarring and scared the shit out of me.

I was locked into a room and told to wait. There was a shitty radio in the room that was playing "Beautiful Day" by U2, and that irony now makes me laugh, but while it was happening, there was nothing funny about it.

A man walked in and looked at my ID, fingerprinted me and took my photo. Since I was never taken into jail when I received my DUI that fateful night, they needed to do it then.

I was also given a huge bright orange badge that said "Inmate" on it, as I was technically an inmate of this jail for the four days I was doing community service. I was to drive only to and from the jail, and be in my hotel room by sundown.

They walked me back to the office to be given my marching orders. I had no idea what they were going to make me do. It could have been picking trash up on the freeway; mopping the jail or who knows what. My mind was racing, and I was just happy to be out of the common area of the jail and in the small office with just a few officers and myself.

One of the officers was looking over a chart of places where they could send me, and then asked me if I was any good at office work. A light turned on inside of me, and I said, "I actually work in an office, and I can do anything you need in here! Filing, inputting, alphabetizing…you name it, I can do it!"

It was the strangest interview I had ever been on in my life, but the office part of me shined brightly, and I got the job!

My task for the day was to staple together hundreds of packets that they would be using for…wait for it…drunk driving classes.

I was so grateful to be safe in the office doing what I knew instead of on the side of the freeway, or in the jail somewhere cleaning.

There was a sobering moment when I walked down the hall to use the restroom, and there was a fellow inmate woman mopping the floor. She had on an orange jumpsuit that had "Inmate" written in bold black letters up and down her leg.

As I passed her to go to the women's restroom, I smiled sheepishly, and her cold dark eyes pierced right through me. I went to open the bathroom door, and she barked at me, "We don't use that restroom. We use the inmate restroom down the hall." She pointed to a door that was much smaller with an orange sign that read "Coed Inmates.".

I croaked out a quick "Thank you" and basically ran down the hallway into the tiny broom closet of a bathroom. Thankfully it was only one stall, but it had no lock on it, so I did my business as quickly as I could, and ran back to the safety of my office chair where I was stapling papers together.

After a few hours of stapling, I had finished, and brought the piles of papers to the officer as I was instructed. It was barely lunchtime; I said, "I'm finished with the packets. I'm a quick study with the stapler."

He looked at me and chuckled a bit, and told me that I could have the rest of the day off, but to make sure I was back at my hotel by sundown, because if I was pulled over again at night, I definitely would be going straight to jail.

I thanked him, and told him I would see him bright and early the next morning.

Each of my four days, I was let off early after finishing one remedial office task, and each day I stopped at the beach, and wrote to the sound of the waves for hours.

I wrote of deep sorrows and regrets for the decisions I made to get myself in this jam. I also wrote of compassion and self-love that I had to find for myself, and finally: I wrote of my steps to true transformation that I was going to bring on in my life now that I know exactly what it is like to have my freedom taken away from me.

We can change our minds in an instant, change our clothes in minutes and change course pretty easily.

True transformation, however, takes time, energy and commitment, and I was truly ready to commit to transformation in life. I made the promise to myself, and the sea to stop drinking and to lose weight, because at the moment, these were the only things I felt I could control in my chaotic life.

I was horrified at myself for letting things get as crazy as they did, and I decided that I needed to stop drinking for a good long time, until I had a new relationship with alcohol, and knew how to control myself with it.

I quit drinking for an entire year, and took a sabbatical from the goth music scene, and started to do more spiritual seeking.

After some clarity and peace soothed the turmoil within my soul, I heard the voice of inner wisdom tell me that it was time to get back to my magical studies and add in more meditation on the Kabbalah Tree of Life to my spiritual tool belt.

I hit the reset button on my life, and started saying no to everyone around me so I could finally say yes to me. Not just yes to another drink or night out in the clubs, but saying yes to my development, healing and transformation.

I secluded myself within my little tiny cabin in the foothills of Altadena, and did the work on myself that my soul was calling out for. I also added to the mix a complete overhaul in my diet, quit drinking all types of soda, cut out sugar and carbs and started to swim laps in the pool I grew up with.

First 20-50 laps. Then I moved up to 75-100 and then I was easily doing 200 laps non-stop multiple times a week, which in time lead to my true physical transformation of losing just over 100 pounds.

The few years prior to this, my life in the cabin was a little crazy with six of my friends moving into the courtyard. There were all night parties, people in and out of my place at all hours, after parties bringing club people, random musicians and hangers on from shows into my healing space.

Again with the dichotomy — spiritual seeker by day, wild club kid by night.

On paper and according to my lease, I still lived alone. In reality, I was right back where I was before the fire, living in a party courtyard with drugs, parties and late nights being the norm. The only difference was that I had a door to a small cottage I could close when I had enough, instead of just a door to a room.

The year of not drinking came as a shock to some of my friends, and sadly, it caused a divide between some of us that never really healed. I suppose it was meant to be, and our time together had expired, but at the time it really hurt that the moment I stopped drinking, in their heads I became off-limits and not worth inviting places.

I was still in the band, and still played shows in bars and clubs, I just chose to drink Shirley Temples instead of shots of Jaeger. Alas, these certain friends couldn't handle hanging out with me when I wasn't up all night drinking with them, so alone I retreated into my spiritual cocoon of meditation my house had become once again.

I spent my free time seeking in spiritual communities, meditating to gain clarity, swimming every chance I got and finally finding myself within the loving embrace of a living Saint.

YOUR HEALING ACTION!

Please log onto
www.thehealingwoods.com/book-bonus/
in order to access your next bonus to further your own personal journey of igniting your light within!

CHAPTER 6

MEETING A LIVING SAINT

Through the Guru the mind becomes purified, thus paving the way towards becoming one with God.

— Amma (Mata Amritanandamayi Devi)

In 1994, two years after graduating high school, I began on a journey of really studying all there was to know about spirituality and religion within the world. The perfect place in which to spark the flame of wisdom about what was out there was my job as a clerk at a New Age Bookstore called Alexandria 2 in Pasadena, California.

Between stocking books and waiting on customers, there was always down time, and I would dust the shelves and find tons of books on religions I had no idea even existed. I learned about Rosicrucianism, Essenes Dead Sea Scrolls, Sikhism and The Gnostics among many others.

I drank all of the information in like a person lost in the desert would water at an oasis.

My life after Alexandria 2 (called A2 for short) became a living Comparative Religions course, and in my free time I studied up on religions that spoke to me, and sought out groups that I could come and experience things like pujas with the Hindus, masses with the

Gnostics and meditations with the Buddhists.

I loved ritual and devotion, and I loved to learn all of the different languages there were within religion in order to say the same thing. I enjoyed having many different ways in which to connect to my Spirit, and seeking the truth became a passion.

Of course, I was 19 when I was working at A2 with a bunch of my partier roommates at the time, so there was also the drinking behind the counter and rolling into work with clothes on from the Goth club the night before aspect of working there.

Even though my life was loudly erratic, I always found time to seek peace.

I always referred back to Alexandria 2, and still do, when I needed a new book to read. There are shelves upon shelves of inspirational books, metaphysical books, meditations, self-help, hundreds of tarot decks and more.

One afternoon in the middle of my year of sobriety at age 30, I had finished the book I was reading, and decided I should go to A2 to see what book was waiting for me there. What new thing could I learn, and add to my spiritual tool belt?

I was minding my own business, pouring through the shelves, when an otherworldly crone whispered behind me, "I see the fairies with you…they miss the forest."

I turned around, and looked into Ambika's crystalline eyes for the first time. She giggled to herself, and disappeared into the back room.

Who was this woman? How did she know about my love of forests and fairies?

I walked up to my friend Carson who was working the front counter, and told him what had happened, and asked him who this creature was.

He laughed and said, "Ambika doesn't just go up and talk to anyone. It means she has something to tell you. I would get a half hour with her if I were you…"

I purchased my half-hour psychic reading with the Crone Fairy Seeress of A2, and sat down in front of her.

I was not new to psychic readings at this point. I had received and given hundreds of Tarot readings, also I had received Astrology readings and even some spirit guide readings, but nothing ever like what I was about to experience.

Ambika's eyes were closed, and there were no pleasantries like,

"Can I get you some water?" or even, "Please have a seat."

No…Ambika just sat there silently, and finally opened her eyes wide like a child and gasped. She took in a huge breath while looking up at the sky and said, "In 25 years of giving these readings I have NEVER seen anything like this!"

Now I was scared.

What was this woman seeing that was THAT huge around me? She was a Spirit Guide reader, and got in touch with the guides around you to tell you what you have around you, and what they have to say to you.

Apparently I had something so huge around me that she hadn't seen in 25 years, and I couldn't wait to hear about who (or what) it was.

"You are surrounded by a grove of huge redwoods on all sides. They miss you, and love when you write for them. They especially like when you sing to them."

My heart was pounding and my gut sank. HOW DID SHE KNOW???

After the initial shock of being completely and utterly seen, I grew excited. I could not wait to hear what sagely advice this Crone Fairy Seeress had to give me.

The half-hour reading turned into an hour, yet it went by in what seemed like five minutes. She introduced me to some Druids who were gathered around me, a thin white line of light in my heart named Illumina and three dragonflies that guided my dreams. She also started to quote things I had actually written within the redwoods. I was crying and sitting opposite this Sage with my heart wide open.

There were so many guides around me; she said that I basically had an army, and then she gasped again, and said, "Ammachi!!" as tears rolled down her face.

"Ammachi?" I said. When I heard the name, there was something that was awoken inside of me. It was as if I knew that hearing that name watered a seed that was lying dormant inside of me.

Ambika went on and on telling me about Ammachi the Hugging Saint, and how she travels around hugging the world and giving Darshan to people. Darshan is the Hindu word for "To see God" and different Indian saints would give Darshan in different ways. Some would sing, some would touch your third eye and some would speak. Amma hugged. It was her way of planting a beautiful seed of devotion to God within you, and helping to clear up some Karmic blockages at the same time.

She also went on a journey with words, telling me how she saw us in a past life worshipping the Hindu Goddess Kali near a huge rock, and that Ammachi is calling me to come back to her.

Truthfully there was SO much information given to me during the reading that I sort of forgot about the whole Ammachi thing, and was focused more on working with Illumina, who was there to help me move through this world as a fairy who was brave enough to come back in this human form. The human form that I despised so.

She also said that I was here to teach the world love.

At the time, I was just getting out of the DUI Hell, the heaviest I have ever been in life (close to 400 pounds) and angry at love. That part of her reading, I dismissed completely.

Little did I know, ten years later that love would be at the core of everything I teach as a Reiki Master and the driving force of all that I do in life. The part I dismissed of this reading, was the most important and to the core thing that was said.

Flash forward a few months from the reading, and I was going about life, and had completely forgotten about the whole Ammachi thing.

One summer night, I woke up from a dream I had of an Indian woman in all white holding me like a baby, and it was one of those dreams that felt like much more than just the subconscious acting out. This felt like it had really happened, and I could even smell a beautiful mixture of sandalwood and rose upon waking up.

Lying in bed, I remembered Ambika's reading, and I immediately got online to see when that Ammachi lady was coming into town.

She had arrived that night.

I knew at that moment that it was fate; Amma was calling me, and I could not ignore the fates with this one.

I called Ambika, and set up a time to go meet Amma with her. We went to the last night of her public program, which is called Devi Bhava. I said yes, even though I had no idea what that meant. (I later learned Devi means Goddess and Bhava means "a state of being" - So Devi Bhava is an all night into the next afternoon celebration where Amma becomes a goddess, and tens of thousands of people come to be hugged by the goddess)

Ambika warned me that it might be a long time before I got to actually hug Amma. There would be tens of thousands of people there, and Amma would be hugging from early evening until afternoon the next day, non-stop.

I was up for the adventure, and met Ambika at her beautiful home in Mt. Washington.

We arrived to the LAX Hilton, and the energy was amazing around this airport hotel that was usually filled with businessmen, pilots, flight attendants and random travelers. This night, it was filled with Indian families in their best saris, a sea of people in white, hippies, artists, yogis and a couple of the mentally unbalanced. Amma hugs everyone.

Amma devotees take over the whole lobby on Devi Bhava, and there were huge lines of people forming all over the place. The smells of delicious Indian food drifted throughout, beautiful tapestries from India covered everything in the mundane Hilton ballroom. The sound of live Indian music filling the electric air.

I had jumped on board the bliss train, and left life as I knew it behind me. This place was like a spiritual rave! There were people dancing and clapping to the Bhajans (Indian devotional music) all through the night and well into the next afternoon; people meditating and crying in piles on the floor; an Indian marketplace set up with colorful saris, jewelry, books and incense. The sights and smells of delicious Indian food being cooked and the sweet aroma of sandalwood-rose wafting in and out of my consciousness.

Where on earth was I?

Was I still in LA?

Did I really just get off the elevator of the LAX Hilton parking garage, and immediately get transported somewhere into India?

I silently thanked myself for saying yes to this, and went on my own journey into the LAX-India portal.

The first moment I set eyes on Amma, I immediately broke down crying. She was so beautiful and glowing. Dressed in an amazing black and red sari, tossing rose petals on people and holding them in her arms while a never ending line of thousands filed up to receive Darshan from her.

In my journeys through LAX-India, I came upon a line of people waiting to receive a mantra from Amma. This intrigued me, so I waited in the line. I was told by multiple people to not be disheartened if Amma does not give me a mantra, since she didn't do it for everyone, and usually won't do it the first time you come to see her.

My inner voice of wisdom told me to wait in line, and I got to watch up close and personal as Amma gave Darshan to people. She was surrounded by her team of twenty people in white making sure that the human which is Amma (a woman in her 50s) had water near her, and wasn't mauled by overzealous devotees and has a fan on her blowing cool air, since the energy around where she gives Darshan is always intense and it can get very warm.

I watched as the man in line in front of me was denied a mantra. Amma looked at him with love in her eyes, but shook a finger back and forth which means, "not yet," and went back to hugging the thousands of people in line to see her.

The man left, and I kneeled next to her; watching as person upon person received Darshan inches from me. Amma had not even looked at me yet. This was fine with me, because the energy coming off of her was palpable, and I was drinking in the love she is with my very soul.

Finally she turned to me, and the most amazing smile exploded on her beautiful face and her eyes got very huge and expressive. She said something I could not understand at all, and the Swami next to her motioned for me to stand up. He gave me a piece of paper and told me to go with the others to learn about my mantra.

In order to even be allowed into the line to ask for a mantra, I had to make three promises:

1) I promise to say it 108 times each day.
2) I promise to not tell anyone what it is.
3) I promise to treat all people I meet as if they were Amma.

I could definitely get behind these promises, so I took my place in a circle of people who just received their mantra, and there were other swamis helping us say them correctly as the mantras were in Sanskrit, and explaining to us what they meant.

Mine was a calling for Divine love, and that was SO perfect for a woman who had grown up hating who she believed to be God, and in turn learning how to hate herself and love.

There are never any accidents at the feet of Amma, and receiving this mantra was my first step in a huge journey of discovery of love for myself and love for God to follow.

A mantra given to you by a Saint is like a seed being planted within the soil of your soul, and so I had the seed of Divine love planted within me. Every time you repeat your mantra within devotion, you water the seed, thus whatever your mantra is for will grow within your life.

I decided to turn on the hose of devotion and bought myself a mala to do my mantra with. I was also told that I could have Amma bless the mala when I received my hug from her, so I did.

Sometime around 6am the next day, it was my turn to receive Darshan.

I was high on real Indian chai, excitement for Darshan, and the amazing energy emanating from everyone in the room who were mirrors for the Divine energy flowing from Amma.

I took my place in line, and slowly moved up the Darshan line. I had my mala in hand, and was saying my mantra as I got closer and closer to her. The tears were welling up in my eyes, and my inner voice was calling to Amma silently, asking her to help me love myself and to heal my heart. "Heal my heart" replaced my mantra for the moment that I was being hugged.

It was such a blur, and the energy and warmth I felt as I was being hugged, reminded me a lot of what I felt as I was having my out of body experience in the burn ward almost a decade back.

I also later learned that on Devi Bhava, Amma was taking on the aspects of a certain goddess, and the color of her sari told of which goddess she was that night. Black and Red is Kali, and that first meeting with Amma as Kali was just the precursor to a long beautiful relationship of growth and transformation with Kali-Amma.

Kali grew to be a very important goddess for me, as she is the fierce mother goddess of time and death. She cuts away anything in your way to what you deserve in life with the sword she carries, and is wonderful to use for protection.

Throughout the next decade, I experienced many miracles and transformative times with my Guru. There were times when I swear she read my mind as I was being held in her arms for Darshan.

One particular retreat I did with Amma when I was around age 35, I had huge amounts of debt left over from the fire, DUI and poor decisions with money as a young adult and I received some horrible news that I was being taken to court by a creditor. This caused me to spiral into the never-ending pit of anxiety and fear.

I decided to use my time with my Guru to an advantage, and held an offering of a pumpkin that I had grown from seed, and put all of my fear and sadness over this news from the creditor into it.

I moved slowly up to Amma in the Darshan line; I was crying and speaking to Amma in my head about how scared I was of the court case, and how I really wanted all of the debt and creditors to leave my life. I was ready to be released from the karmic debt, which was rooted within the fire.

I finally arrived right in front of Amma, and smelled the sandalwood-rose, which entered my senses like a kiss from an angel. With shaking hands, I gave my pumpkin full of worries to her as an offering.

Usually Amma would take each offering she was given with care and pass it over to her helpers who put it in baskets for safe keeping. This particular pumpkin of fear, she looked at and then looked back at me and threw up so high over her shoulder that it almost hit the ceiling. She laughed and shook her head and hugged me longer than I have ever been hugged while receiving Darshan.

I took this to mean that I was not to fear, and that this too shall pass, and even though it felt as if I would never get out from under that more than $40,000 worth of debt, I eventually did; exactly when I was supposed to. I felt cared for by The Universe through the whole process of paying it off.

One of the most transformational times with Amma was my first Kali Puja fire which was held in the mountains of Santa Barbara overlooking the ocean in the distance with beautiful oak groves all around us.

The retreat was done within silence except for chanting and singing Bhajans as an offering to The Divine. I was so excited to experience hiking, meditation, chanting and living within the energy of Amma with a large group of people who were my spiritual tribe.

This was another one of those things that I couldn't help but say yes to upon hearing about it, even though at the time it didn't make sense for me to go, because I didn't really know anyone else going, and I was very new to the Amma community.

The voice of inner wisdom said yes…so I booked my stay within this retreat, and lost myself within the oak groves, bhajans, meditations and silent nature hikes.

On the last night, I awoke to the song of a Tibetan singing bowl at 4am. The full moonlight was cascading on the wooden floors showing the wind dance of the oaks watching over our cabin. The smell of last night's camphor and sandalwood-rose incense still permeated the air.

I immediately felt the rush of energy coursing through me…this was the morning…THIS was the grand finale of the week long silent meditation retreat…this was my Kali Puja, where my brothers and sisters and I will burn out of our lives that which no longer serves in order to make room for that which we desire and deserve this lifetime.

We walked in silence into the cold darkness; we were guided by moonlight and smoke from the Puja Fire.

Waiting for us in the middle of a beautiful oak grove was Ma Devi dressed in her finest white Sari prayed over by Saints and sewn with love in India by the devotees of Amma.

Again sandalwood-rose filled the air as she began to clap, chant and dance around the fire burning oils in lamps; throwing flower petals in water, pouring milk over statues and calling in the omnipresent ones.

Her beautiful dance was accompanied by the sound of tabla drums, Indian bells, a vibraphone humming tunes of devotion and all of us were using our voices for the first time in a week.

Within our chanting we called out to God/ Goddess/ Buddha/ Krishna/ The Universe/ The Flying Spaghetti Monster…whoever we saw fit to thank for releasing us from the binds of the past in order for us to flow freely down the river into the vast beautiful ocean of the future.

The Bhajans continually grew with intensity; our voices getting louder and louder as we sang Hindi in call-and-response style until after an hour or so, we weren't sure who was calling and who was responding. Instead we just called out using our voices in any language that came out of us.

Drum beats getting faster, voices louder, fires raging until it finally happened: Ma Devi arose from her perch at the head of the Puja Fire and asked for us all to come up one at a time and receive Prasad, which is a blessed food to eat and know that all that we have prayed to receive during the Puja is well on its way to us.

I was ecstatic at this point with the hours of meditation, singing, clapping and spiritual energy flying around our group of twenty. With tears of joy running down my face, I crawled up to Ma Devi with my hands cupped to receive her blessing.

A delicious mixture of rice, honey, raisins and love was put into my hand, and I ate it; knowing that all that I desired and deserved was flying towards me at warp speed.

As I turned from Ma Devi, and made my way back to the fire…the sunrise caught my eye, and I silently laid in the grass allowing the new dawn to wash over me, and rested within its Divine light as the smell of sandalwood-rose filled the air, my heart and my soul.

Life was never the same after that Kali Puja.

Two weeks after I returned from Santa Barbara, the advertising agency I was a buyer at closed their doors, and I had experienced a complete release from the job that had been standing in the way of my life's work.

Instead of getting on Monster.com or LinkedIn trying to network my way into another position in the Purgatory that was the Media Industry, I decided to go further within my Reiki studies and become a Reiki Master. At the same time, I also decided to begin my journey with body work within massage school.

On paper, I looked amazing for a soul-wrenching job within the advertising industry. I was even asked by an ex-employer to come back for much more than I was making when I left.

Someone who had not heard the calling of her heart may have seen this as the Universe opening a door to give back what it took. Since I was making decisions with my heart, I saw it as a danger sign, and ran the other way into the doors of a Holistic Massage School.

I was single, had no kids and was living in my tiny cabin in the hills of Altadena for $600 a month, and so I was able to live off of unemployment while I took classes to become a licensed massage therapist.

I was so excited to make my dream of singing, writing and healing for a living come true. I took many trips to the forests and shores of the Pacific Northwest during breaks in my schooling.

For the first time in my life, I felt as if I owned my own time, and was able to explore the mist-covered forests and beaches, without the sinking feeling of having to go back to a desk job once the fun was over.

Instead, I was excited to come back home to learn more about the body and how to work with the hundreds of muscles and tissues it contains.

I was going to be a massage therapist, and move into a heart based business after running away screaming from the stress the sales-based business of the media industry.

At every beach I explored up and down the coast, I would walk up to the edge of the water where the waves came in and out, and write with a piece driftwood in the sand, "Singing Writing Healing."

I'd look up to the Universe and ask it to use me as its tool through these three passions in my life.

As the waves rushed in to take my sand written prayers away, I felt they blessed me with their presence and whispered wisdom to me through the song of the sea foam.

It only made sense that I also move further down my path of learning to becoming a Reiki Master.

I found my next Reiki master at my massage school, who I took a Reiki 2 class with. She was newer at it, and was offering classes at a very low rate, which at the time made my small unemployed bank account very happy.

I had very low rent and lived within my means during this transition, but I was under the shadow of a huge amount of debt from the fire, and was still trying to make payments on that through this, so any break on prices was a blessing to me.

How amazingly blessed did I feel when she told me during my Reiki 2 attunement that her Reiki Guides told her that I was already a Master, and to attune me to the Reiki Master/Teacher level.

I could not even believe my luck! The Universe completely blew the doors wide open to me becoming a Master, and I couldn't wait to get started writing my classes!

I later found out that it was a huge disservice in the end, because she never taught me anything about being a Master. I had training for Reiki 1 and 2, and did my own research on how to be a Reiki Master with other Masters around me who were friends of mine.

I wanted to be sure that I was giving my students everything they should receive within a Reiki Master class, so I ended up having to retake the Reiki Master class with a different Master in the future, but I suppose everything happens for a reason, and she came when she did to give me the quick ride to Reiki Master I needed then.

This time of not working was one of the busiest in my life. I was in the middle of writing a new album with the band, going to massage school full-time and building a network of healers around me.

Within the band, I was connecting with people and networking with other bands and club promoters. I booked us up and down the coast and pretty much everywhere there was to play in Los Angeles that was not pay-to-play, since we decided early on that we would never be a band who pays to play any of the clubs we would bring fans into.

I also started to do Tarot readings in between sets at shows and at goth clubs to supplement my income. To this day, I still work with some of the people I did fifteen minute readings for in the swirling energy of the goth clubs. I didn't know it back then, but I had just started building my list for The Healing Woods as Demonika Darkly.

The band and I were growing as people, and so our music was growing, and my lyrics were moving far away from the darkness they were in the beginning.

I would spend hours driving around the forests and beaches of Humboldt County listening to recordings of our new songs over and over again. When I felt the lyrics I was pregnant with were crowning, I would pull over, find a tree to crawl into the root system of, cry and write a full song's lyrics in minutes.

The words literally flowed from my soul; no brain needed.

Having this foreshadowing of how beautiful life could be really gave me the fuel I needed to keep this vision alive, even through getting another job in the Media Industry once school was over.

I had a wake up call from The Universe with my decade old Jetta breaking down in the Bay Area in the middle of the band's tour. I knew it was my sign to get back into the workforce now that my training in massage therapy and Reiki were completed.

This was a beautiful way that Reiki came to rescue me in the depths of Oakland with my credit cards maxed and a transmission blown at 2am after a gig.

After I got my car towed to the nearest gas station, and was returned safely home to my friend's house; I cried. A lot. Hot tears filled with fear and frustration. How could I be so close to the dream life I knew I was born to live, yet have this huge hurtle show up right after playing one of the best shows of my life?

Once I was done crying and feeling sorry for myself, I grabbed the keys to my completely dead car, and sent Reiki to it. I envisioned myself getting home safely, and the bill for the repair being under $200, so I could still have some money for gas, since that was all I had left in my checking account.

Reiki is energy and can help cars, electronics and other things that run on energy. It is also a great way to manifest an ending for the good of all. For the good of my cats, my wallet and my family; I needed to get back to LA safe and sound so I could look for a job.

I fell asleep sending Reiki to my car, and awoke to a dull grey Oakland morning, and set out to see how bad the damage was with my car.

The guy put it on the computer of doom that tells you what is wrong with your car, and my worst fears were realized when he said, "It's the transmission, and I don't work on Volkswagens, so you're going to have to go to the dealership."

A transmission at a Volkswagen dealership is around $6,500.

I literally had $200 to my name, and absolutely no credit cards as I was still trying to pay down all of the thousands I owed from the fire. I had to cancel all of my cards as part of the debt consolidation program I was in.

My next unemployment check would not come for another two weeks, and it would be somewhere in the neighborhood of $800. Nowhere near enough to get my car running again.

My heart sank as I cried, and called another tow truck driver to come get me.

"A lot of good that Reiki did me…" I sighed as I got into the tow truck driver's cab, and told him to take me to the dealer.

"Why would you want to go there?" he said to which I said, "I am not from here, and have no idea where to go that will work on a Volkswagen transmission. The guy told me to go there, but if you have another place in mind, I am totally open."

"My buddy has a transmission shop, and he works on Volkswagens. Let's go there and see what he can do for you." and with that my hope was instantly restored, and I switched my intentions to focus on the bill being under $200 as we drove through the misty streets of Oakland to his buddy's place.

I told his buddy that I didn't have more than $200, and that I needed the car to drive me all the way back to Los Angeles. He understood, and told me he would call me to give me an update once he figured out what was happening under the hood.

A few hours later I received a call from Buddy, and he said, "She's all ready to go. I put a good Band-Aid on her, and she'll get you home, but you will need to get some deeper work done after you get home. Oh…and that will be $150. Gives you $50 for gas to get home."

Buddy was my new hero as I cried tears of joy this time. I picked up my car and drove south on the I-5, sending Reiki to my car the whole time until I safely arrived back in LA.

Now that I was home, the cold reality set in that the album was written, the tour was done, and I had completed my schooling and was a massage therapist and Reiki Master. I now needed to get that job again to pay the bills in order for me to build my work within The Healing Woods.

This was where my next Reiki manifesting miracle came into my life.

I did not want to go back to work in West LA, where most of the Media Industry jobs were. That meant an hour and a half commute there and back each day. That meant spending three hours a day; 15 hours a day a week; 780 hours a year in the stop-and-go traffic surrounded by angry drivers and a shit show of road rage shown to me weekly.

I needed a job, but I needed my soul more.

I had my mind set on an advertising agency in Pasadena. An easy eight-minute commute from me.

This particular agency worked with all non profit organizations which were helping women fight breast cancer, helping third world countries find clean water and helping feed starving children.

I was definitely more into this than the McDonalds, Lexus and makeup products I helped find ad space on the television shows I never watched because I didn't even own a TV.

I went to go talk to the manager I knew at the ad agency, and was told that there were no open positions, and that hardly anyone ever left because people loved working there so much.

The person I was speaking to had been there over twenty years, and most of the buyers over a decade. Even the assistants stayed put, which is very much not the norm of an advertising agency.

This did not derail me. I sent Reiki to the situation. I visualized myself driving to work and turning into the parking lot and going up the six floors and walking to my desk.

I passed by the building a lot in my travels, since it was just a handful of miles from my house, and every time I did, I sent Reiki to the building telling it that I would soon be working there.

I didn't even reach out to any of the West LA agencies, because I literally could never make the calls. It felt like calling Death to come and giving him a roadmap to my front door. I would rather be homeless than be stuck in the commuting Hell again. Twelve years of it was more than enough for me.

About two weeks later, I received a call from the agency I was focusing on. The manager called and asked if I was still available for a position there.

I could not believe what I was hearing. "YES!!!!" I practically screamed, and it was done. I was offered a position at the agency even though weeks before I was told there was nothing available.

The backstory is that one of the buyers went to visit her family in the Philippines and something went wrong with her paperwork, and she was not allowed to come back to the United States.

At first I felt horrible. Did I create this drama in her life? I didn't mean for anything bad to happen to anyone; I just wanted so badly to be in an agency that was close to me and had clients that made a difference in the world.

I later found out that she wasn't really very happy in the US. She couldn't find a boyfriend, and really wanted to get married and have a family. Once she was in the Philippines, she found her husband and was happier than she'd ever been here.

Reiki works for the good of all. You can never send Reiki to a situation to make someone lose something just so you gain. It works only if what you are focusing on will help all people involved.

I had a new job.

I had more time to devote to my Healing Woods work instead of driving the fifteen hours a week to a job.

I had so much respect and honor for Reiki and how it can completely and totally transform your life.

I couldn't wait to get focused on taking paying clients, and see how far I could go with building my own business with the extra time I had.

I worked 9-5pm at the advertising agency, and then saw clients and went to healing fairs and networking events 5-9pm. Then, I sometimes had shows with the band after from 9-2am; no rest for the wicked.

Life was the busiest it had ever been with full-time work, building a business and still booking, promoting and playing in the band weekly, but I wouldn't have it any other way.

I am happy I allowed myself to take the Leap of Faith of not looking for another job right away. Because of this I was able to experience all of the magic of learning a new healing modality and experiencing the magic of using Reiki to transform my life.

Life is meant for living to its fullest…not just existing.

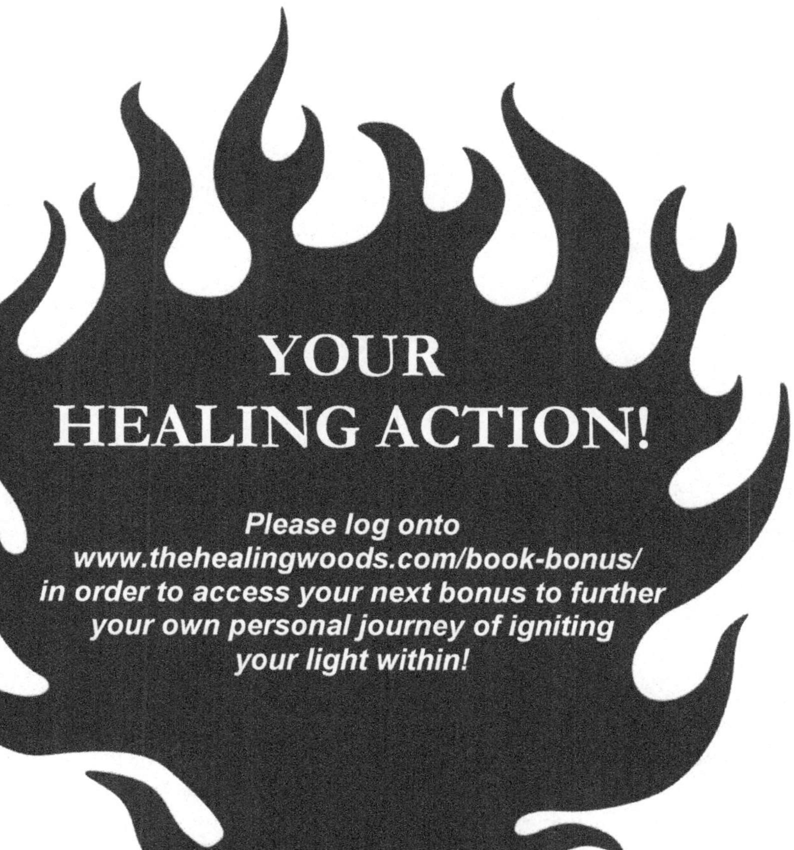
YOUR
HEALING ACTION!
Please log onto
www.thehealingwoods.com/book-bonus/
in order to access your next bonus to further
your own personal journey of igniting
your light within!

CHAPTER 7

BECOMING ABHAYADA

A wise man lights a candle while fools are busy cursing the darkness.

— Seth Czerepak

It was 2007, I was in my early 30's and the band was going strong, and I found myself immersed within a scene I was no longer feeling, yet it fueled the band's ability to play live on stage. I found myself at goth clubs, at live shows of fellow goth bands, and networking within the heavy energies of all involved within the scene.

As a teenager, if you would have told me that in my 30's, I would be the lead singer of an up-and-coming Goth Band, play a Goth Day at Disneyland called Bat's Day and play sometimes weekly in Goth clubs I would have cried with excitement.

As that 30-something-year old stuck within the trappings of the scene, my soul was crying out to be released from the scene's oppressive walls.

I did, and still do have a huge place in my heart for the scene, and all of the beautiful music that has been created within it.

To this day, once in awhile, I will still go out to a Goth club to dance, or put on an old album that brings me back to that beautiful time where I felt free, flowing around the dance floor in a leather corset and a flowing black lace dress. As fun as all of that was, I had gone through another huge shift after meeting Amma, and my time learning and growing within the dark had ended. I was ready to sprout up through the darkness of the earth, and grow into the sunlight.

My roots are within that scene, and the pain I was feeling as a teenager within that self-hate and longing to die, was the fertilizer for my growth.

Roots are meant to be kept in the dark; they receive nourishment from the soil within the dark. Once they are ready for the sun…the sprout of growth makes its brave journey from the darkness of the soil into the glory of the sunlight and air.

My sprout was growing rapidly, and very bored of the same old clubs, same old music and same old darkness.

At this point I was singing lyrics in Hindi weaved into the lyrics of the band's music, playing Indian bells and Tibetan singing bowls within our music, going to healing events, drumming circles, Reiki shares and meditation retreats. These places allowed me to sparkle and shine as brightly as I wanted, and once I tasted the sweet nectar of the light; I was never able to go back to the same old dark scene again.

My vision was for the band to transcend playing dive bars and Goth clubs, and play outdoor festivals, art shows, spiritual events and other gatherings within the light. The few outdoor art shows and festivals we played were amazing. Our music was never your basic Goth music, and so we were totally welcomed and it was beautiful to see smiling people with children watching us, and enjoying our music.

I was asked to join the Ammachi Satsang Music Group, which helped teach me to sing Sanskrit and Bhajans, as about 90-percent of the music we performed was in Hindi.

One of the most memorable times the Amma group performed was for Devi Bhava when Amma was at the LAX Hilton.

Shashi, who is my spiritual grandmother, a wisp of a 70-year-old woman with bright red hair, a gypsy's traveling soul and the ability to play the harmonium with the best of them, heard me sing at the Kali Puja in the oak grove, and asked me to join their group. She said, "Your soulful voice needs to be heard!" and so it was done.

I told her about my band, and how we had a song especially for Amma, and she asked for it, and then learned it on harmonium. The music group was comprised of tabla drums, Indian bells, harmonium, bass, flute, guitar and many beautiful singers all devoted to praying to The Divine Mother through song.

This amazing group was now doing a version of my band's Ammachi song, and that song was being performed directly for Amma in front of ten thousand people in the LAX Hilton Grand Ballroom!

I could not believe this huge gift from The Universe; to be able to sing the lyrics I wrote for Amma *to* Amma!

Ten thousand people was the most I had ever performed in front of, but with Amma there, everyone else disappeared, and it was just the LA Satsang Amma Music Group Amma and I. The song was performed in call and response style, which means, I sang a line, and everyone in the room would sing it back to me.

This was the first time I heard my lyrics echoed back to me by thousands of people and I shook with joy and tears fell down my face. It was the most connected I have ever felt to an audience in my whole life. These lyrics were written as a prayer of thanks to Amma, so to have thousands of people join in my prayer was one of the most fulfilling moments I have ever had within singing.

It was much different than the post punk version Demonika and the Darklings did, and my whole body and voice were electric as the LAX Hilton Ballroom responded back my first line, "Through my darkest hate your love shines through as I crawl on my hands and knees to you."

In true Bhajans call-and-response style, the song starts out quite slow and picks up speed at each verse until it ends in a fast-paced beat with the whole room clapping and singing, "Aum Shanti Shanti Shantihi!"

As they are repeating this over and over, I am freestyling calling out to Amma, and holding full bodied tones that fluttered and changed notes erratically. I was never taught to sing in this style, it just erupted within me and my throat chakra literally opened up and released it while singing to my Guru.

I had no idea what was coming out, but it was Amma's name, and the voice was strong and powerful and echoed above the thousands singing in the Hilton. Amma stopped for a moment when she was in the middle of hugging thousands and looked right at me; she pointed at me and smiled so brightly as I was singing out her name in tears.

I felt her eyes in my heart.

I felt her even more strongly within my soul, and from that day forward my voice was never the same. Hindi and spiritual growth found their way even more intensely into every lyric I wrote and performed on stage with the band.

Ammachi

Lyrics written by Kristin Dwan

Through my darkest hate your love shines through,
As I crawl on my hands and knees to you.
Feeling things I've never felt allowed within,
Abolished of past Karmic Traps and sins.

Aum Amma
Aum Ammachi
Aum shanti shanti shantihi,
Shanti shanti shine within me!

Feeling silence where I once hid rage,
Setting my heart and soul free of their cage.
That cage of doubt I festered through,
Was blown wide open thanks to you.

Aum Amma
Aum Ammachi
Aum shanti shanti shantihi,
Shanti shanti shine within me!

With new eyes it's me I finally see,
As well as who I left to finally be.
What I stop begins what I start,
Forgetting mind and using heart.

Aum Amma
Aum Ammachi
Aum shanti shanti shantihi,
Shanti shanti shine within me!

That same retreat, I made my way to Amma, and asked for a spiritual name.

I had been with her for some years now, and felt it was time to shed Demonika and become whoever it was I was growing into, and she needed a new name.

I was on my knees breathing in the sandalwood-rose that emanates from Amma's very pores, and crying in joy of getting named by my Guru. The Divine bliss I felt this night was the highest level I have yet to experience.

The line of hundreds in front of her waiting for her hug, and the swamis behind her holding space, and asking her for the people who were requesting a name was an intoxicating dance to witness. I was in a sort of daze just staring at Amma's profile; she was hugging and listening to the prayers of the thousands.

The atmosphere was absolutely buzzing with the dance in front of me; the live Indian music blaring in the background with the whole Hilton singing and clapping, but at the moment Amma turned to me to look in my eyes, all of the noise disappeared. It was just Amma and I together in the silence, and she whispered my spiritual name into my ear with her beautiful raspy voice, "Abhayada."

Abhayada. (Pronounced Ah-**bye**-a-duh)

I looked at the swami, who gave me a piece of paper with it written on it, and taught me how to say it. He also told me what it meant, "One who gives shelter fearlessly." At hearing this, I totally lost it and started bawling.

That is so perfect for me. In my healing work I am never afraid to go deep with my clients, and really carve out the deep, dark root that festers within them to any trauma, self-hate or illness they had.

In my life, I am always facing the demons and slaying the dragons, and I do so without fear.

Abhayada.

I sat down to do my mantra for the first time as Abhayada, and next to me was a beautiful Indian Elder who said to me, "I watched you get your name. What did Amma name you?" I replied, "Abhayada."

Upon hearing this her eyes lit up, and she exclaimed, "OH! You must be a healer. Amma only names people who were meant to heal, Abhayada!"

Upon hearing this, all of my doubts and fears about my decisions to become a Reiki Master and Massage Therapist flew out of existence.

Who was I with my doubts and fears to get in the way of my true soul's calling as a healer?

Who was I to waste anymore time hiding behind the façade of Demonika within the Goth scene?

It was time for the light of Abhayada to shine brightly and unfettered.

I was finally released from my dark and angry past into the excitement of what the light had in store for me.

In the coming months, the band was transforming as well, and made some changes; adding in guitar to compliment the violin, a new drummer, and deciding to play during the light of day at art shows and spiritual events.

With this shift the band was going through, our music was definitely shifting too, and I wanted to shed Demonika from Demonika and the Darklings, and just be The Darklings. My stage name went from Demonika to Abhayada.

I always sent out emails to our fans with news about upcoming shows, new songs and deep, introspective stuff about the lyrics and what they meant.

As Demonika Darkly, I always signed the e-mail: Darkly Yours, Demonika.

Now that Abhayada was writing the emails it switched to: Yours in the Light, Abhayada.

The shift was not understood nor liked my some fans, but I was ready for that, and frankly after everything I had experienced in life, I did not care in the least.

I knew that whoever left because they didn't understand my new phase in life would be replaced by new fans who shined with me, instead of shadowing against me.

It was the same lesson I learned when I stopped drinking and lost some party friends in order to make room for my spiritual tribe. I also stopped hiding within darkness and lost some Goth fans in order to make room for new everyday people fans.

I also immersed myself very heavily in the Amma culture and learned to meditate even more deeply in IAM Meditation, which Amma created. It integrates yoga, chakras, mantra and meditation. I continued to focus on being at healing events and continued with the break from drinking while losing even more weight.

Now that I was becoming even more of a hermit, the divide was showing itself not just with basic party friends, but even with good friends I had living within the courtyard who I had previously partied until dawn with many a night who did not like that I quit drinking.

I literally had one friend I had since high school tell me he liked most of the changes I had made, but hated that I didn't drink anymore.

I noticed that they slowly stopped inviting me out with them, and the divide between these people I had toured the San Gabriel Valley with, living in different homes together was set in place.

Apparently our friendships could survive me burning down a house, but they could not survive me changing my life for the better and moving on from the party lifestyle we all so diligently shared.

I was still singing in the band, and still in clubs and bars, but I was just not drinking. I was still me, and still fun and still willing to go to the bars and clubs to meet them where they were at, but something about my sobriety, meditation and spirituality drove them away.

It hurt a lot in the beginning, but what I now realize about that time is that it was all about them and their own travels, and not about me. I was a mirror for some of them, and they have all grown up and most are married and even have kids now. I just grew up a bit sooner is all. The Universe forced it on me, and for that, I am ever grateful.

My year of sobriety was one of the most clear and beautiful as far as growth goes that I have ever had.

I focused on myself, and lost more weight with swimming and dietary changes.

I was feeling amazing, meeting new people who would grow to be friends just as close as those that were over their expiration date. I was looking sexy and falling even more deeply in love with me and going on adventures with lovers and within love.

All was beautiful except for the growing pain inside of my gut that wouldn't go away that I suffered through for 9 months.

While I was working on my Solar Plexus within a Self-Reiki session one day, I felt a flutter happen in my stomach, and it started growing into a jumping feeling right where my gut pain was felt. Before I knew it, my whole body was shaking uncontrollably, and my teeth were even chattering.

This went on for about an hour, and it got to the point where I was literally shuddering and shaking uncontrollably. I was wondering if I was having full on convulsions, and I was just about ready to call

911.

I heard Amma's voice in my head say, "Lay down child, and go to the doctor tomorrow and demand they look inside of you."

At that moment, I curled up in fetal position under my covers in the dark and continued to shake and said my mantra until my body calmed down. I finally passed out at dawn.

The next day, I went to the doctor and when she asked how I was doing, I told her that I was not feeling any better, and in fact things seemed to be getting worse. The pain in my abdomen felt as if it was on fire, every time I urinated I had to brace myself and take a deep breath because it felt as if I was passing fire and shards of glass put together. I also had no energy whatsoever.

She again wanted to put me on an even stronger antibiotic, and at that point I screamed at her, "Enough with these useless pills, get me into a CAT Scan and figure out what the hell is happening inside of me!!"

She agreed to a CAT Scan, even though she had to say that she thought I was overreacting, and I went for my scan a few days later.

A few hours after my scan, I was called by the doctor's office, and the conversation went something like this:

Me: "Hello?"

Them: "May I speak to Kristin?"

Me: "This is she."

Them: "This is regarding your CAT Scan results. Are you feeling OK? Are you in a great amount of pain?"

Me: "No. I am not feeling OK at all. I have been in huge amounts of abdominal pain for nine months now, and kept telling my doctor this."

Them: "We need you to check into Arcadia Methodist Hospital as soon as you can today. Please do not be too active, as you have a large abscess in-between your Sigmoid Colon and Bladder, which if it erupts, your system will become septic, and this could lead to death."

I had just finished swimming 100 laps in my mom's pool. For nine months I was being very active in the gym and swimming using my core to lose this weight.

I said a prayer of thanks to The Universe for my abscess not erupting and for finally figuring out what this fiery pain was inside of my gut. In a daze I packed an overnight bag, called my mom and drove myself to the hospital to check into my home for the next month.

I find it very interesting that the date I checked myself in was the 10-year anniversary of the fire: August, 23rd, 2008. I had planned to get a tattoo of a phoenix that day, but instead I started another adventure of becoming a phoenix within yet another hospital.

My diagnosis was Diverticulitis. In a nutshell, my colon had small pockets inside of it called diverticula, and when a nut or seed gets lodged in there, it can cause the colon to become irritated and inflamed. If it does not get treated properly, it can become infected, and begin a chain reaction of horrible things around and within the colon.

Mine was inflamed and infected for a good nine months by now, so I had the added bonus of a fistula in between my colon and bladder. A fistula is basically a bridge that grows between two organs, and since nothing was treated properly for so long, my sigmoid (large) colon and bladder were now connected, and emptying out into one another.

This was why it felt as if I was passing fire and glass every time I urinated, and I was stopped up completely as my colon basically shut down from the trauma happening within it.

My surgeon tried his best to fix me without cutting me open.

My first week was spent bed bound in the hospital with hardcore antibiotics administered intravenously around the clock. The pain was not as bad as it was earlier, but my fistula and abscess were fighting back, and proving hard to beat with just medication.

The next step was to take a huge syringe, and stick it through my bellybutton to try to drain the abscess.

They used a local anesthetic, so I was still completely awake for this, and felt exactly where the needle was in my organs. I felt, heard and witnessed the vile liquid being suctioned out of my Solar Plexus.

Within 24 hours of this attack on my insides, the abscess fought back hardcore. I woke up in the most intense pain I'd ever felt. It was as if the nine months of pain were rolled up into one, and I was given it all at once that day.

The preparations for a Colon Resection surgery were underway, and the doctor informed me that there was an 80-percent chance that I would be waking up with a colostomy bag since the abscess was so large. He left some informational paperwork with my mom and I about things to know about having a colostomy bag.

I completely disregarded the paperwork, and instead of reading that, I began using Reiki to imagine how excited I would be to wake up after the surgery completely intact without the need for a colostomy bag. I also enlisted all of the healers I knew to send me Reiki, do candle work and make offerings to any gods or goddesses they worked with to have this bagless colon resection go well.

I did Reiki on myself within the hospital bed, on the way down the shiny white halls to the operating room, as the mask was put on my face, and I counted down backwards from 10…9…8…..

The next thing I knew I was awake, and the pain inside my gut was indescribable. A completely different affliction than when I awoke from the skin grafting. That was incredibly painful, but surface.

This pain seemed to come deep within my soul, and was completely overpowering even though I had liquid Morphine running through my veins.

As soon as I could get my mouth working and remembered how to speak, I squinted at the nurse watching over me and hoarsely croaked, "Do I have a bag?"

She smiled at me, and said, "No. The doctor was able to successfully resect two healthy parts of your colon. Here are some ice chips for you."

Those were the most delicious ice chips I had ever tasted, knowing that my body was whole, and I was able to embody the 20-percent chance I was given of escaping the colostomy bag.

The following weeks were a bit touch and go. I was literally unable to bend or move around very well in the hospital bed. I pushed the red button of bliss, which allowed Morphine to flow in my veins as many times as I possibly could. Breathing hurt. Laughing really killed my abdomen, and sneezing made me scream out in pain.

I was literally stapled together. I had an eight-inch incision from my bellybutton to my pelvis, and things were draining out of tubes that were placed all over this area.

The surgeon removed a foot and a half of the infected colon, and I was on a liquid diet that was given to me intravenously since my colon was unable to have anything go through it for the next few weeks.

There was still a chance that I would have to get a bag, if the two healthy parts of my colon did not heal together correctly.

Basically it was a waiting game with my internal organs. I had to first pass gas naturally before they would let me drink liquids, so I had liquids being fed into my veins. Then I had to have a natural bowel movement before they would let me eat solid food.

I had a group of close friends that I had in a text group who kept checking on my healing, and I was literally so overjoyed when I passed gas that I texted all of them to let them know. This meant my colon was starting to heal, and the surgery was a success!

At this point I was allowed to drink soups, smoothies, pudding, and things like that in order to help nature take its course, and hopefully allow for me to have a bowel movement.

About two weeks later, I had my first bowel movement, and cried tears of joy.

This was also the first time I was off of a catheter, and able to freely urinate. The simple things in life that we take for granted are the most complex and daunting when your ability to experience them is taken away.

The first time my bladder was allowed to release into a toilet instead of a catheter was the first time I had urinated without intense pain in over nine months. Just that alone caused me to hug my surgeon while I profusely thanked him and felt so much relief that I was finally not writhing in pain every time I went to the restroom.

The pain became less and less as the days passed on in my Morphine haze.

I had nothing but time to write, and within this Morphine haze I was able to get right to the root of why this was happening to me.

The part of my colon that had to be removed was energetically filled with all of the unexpressed anger and rage towards my parents' divorce, old hatred of myself, and intense depression of my teen years.

On the 10th anniversary of the fire burning everything away from my outside that was not for my soul's greatest good; the root of that anger, depression and trauma had to be literally dug up and cut out of me.

I felt lighter. Not just because I had lost twenty pounds from the month of liquid diet and the removal of parts of me, but lighter in an energetic and emotional way.

It was as if when I died and came back to life in the Grossman Burn Ward; my soul did all that it could with the body it was placed back into to heal the past emotional trauma. A decade later, it came to a point where it needed help with releasing the root of that anger, and that is where the surgeon's knife came in.

After living through this, I was again a completely different person. I was not walking around in hidden anger and depression. I was so happy to not only be alive, but to be able to be complete and whole with my bladder and colon working properly and painlessly.

After I healed and strengthened, I allowed men into my life again, and I started dating in a totally different way than before the surgery. I allowed them into my heart, not just my bed.

I had a new belief in love because I had a new belief in me.

While I was being ripped open and healing from my latest rebirth, the band was still meeting and creating new songs for me to write words to.

My first lyrics became still to this day one of my favorite songs that we created, called Morphine Dreams:

Morphine Dreams

Music by The Darklings
Lyrics by Kristin Dwan

Cut through the muscle to release the pain,
Since opening up I have not been the same.
Let go and let love and forget about fear,
My awakening to pain is finally here.

Morphine dreams silence scar tissue screams.

When death is born within my lifetime,
The roots that being sprouts from are mine.
Soar in the sky on wings so new,
My awakening to love is something true.

Love flow from me as I rip at the seams.

Change will come,
Change will go,
Love will flood,
Love will flow,
I have asked…I now know.

Morphine dreams silence scar tissue screams.
Love flow from me as I rip at the seams.

This was the song we always started shows with.

This was also the song that started me doing Reiki on stage as we played. It had a long intro where each instrument came in staggered before I started singing.

We usually opened our sets with this song, and during the time the intro was playing I had my back to the audience doing Reiki. I'd start on myself, and then my band, and as I turned around to finally sing, I spread the Reiki to the whole venue and everyone in it.

This is around that time that things sped up quite beautifully for the band and we were attracting bigger and better shows.

This is also around the time that I knew life could not keep going the way it was.

Having this second rebirth showed me that I still definitely had things to release, and now that I had released a part of my inner organs…people and situations seemed much easier to free myself from.

I no longer said yes to things I felt obligated to go to just because I had known the person for so long. I no longer ran myself ragged trying to be there for everyone. I started to say no to people in order to say yes to me and what I needed in life, and it felt amazing and easy to do.

After a few years of clearing these people and situations out of my life, I knew the next thing I had to release myself from was my beloved cocoon/home of 14 years.

This butterfly's wings were ready to soar onto bigger and better.

YOUR HEALING ACTION!

Please log onto www.thehealingwoods.com/book-bonus/ in order to access your next bonus to further your own personal journey of igniting your light within!

CHAPTER 8

2012…A PARADIGM SHIFT

And the day came when the risk
to remain tight in a bud was more painful
than the risk it took to blossom.

— Anais Nin

As soon as I knew I was finished with my beautiful but insanely tiny cabin in the courtyard surrounded by trees, I began making my list of what I wanted to manifest in my new home.

Even though it scared the crap out of me, I knew I needed to have a two bedroom home in order to build The Healing Woods into a real business where people besides friends and family could come to see me.

The cottage I lived in wasn't even big enough for me to open up my massage table in, so I always had to travel to people's homes in order to offer them Reiki or Massage, or have my friends lay on the couch as I did Reiki on them.

Not very professional at all, and I felt the deep calling within me to start looking at The Healing Woods as my next era of work.

I spent far too many years merely having a job, it was time for my soul's work to get some of my time and energy, and have a beautiful home in which to grow.

The job that I was at was allowing me to work more hours at The Healing Woods, because of my non-existent commute, which meant I had an extra 15 hours a week I was able to take back from the freeways of Los Angeles and put into building my business and servicing my small but growing client list.

I learned a lot about advertising, selling, client service and speaking with confidence in my corporate jobs, and I had a decade worth of experience marketing the band and building an email list of fans with that, so building a client list for The Healing Woods was going more quickly than I expected, and word of mouth was growing my list without me having to do any advertising.

This was a sign from The Universe that it was time for me to get serious about having a whole room in a house that was dedicated to only The Healing Woods, and even though I was a single girl living on her own, I committed to a 2-bedroom house.

I had no idea where my house was, or when it would be coming. I just knew that it was on its way, so I had better be ready!

It's amazing how much junk you can collect after 14 years in a house. I moved into that tiny place with just enough stuff to fill my car in one trip right after the fire, and I was leaving with enough to fill a large U Haul.

I went through and did a huge purge of stuff that no longer served me, and actually started packing up boxes of stuff that I could do without for a few months, so I could put the energy of moving out into The Universe, so it knew I was serious and ready to manifest the house and make the move.

I looked in the papers and online and went to see a few houses, but they weren't really what I wanted. I didn't feel them in my bones.

I decided that I would take the upcoming Full Moon to get very clear on what it was that I wanted within my new home, and it was perfect that I would just happen to be in Humboldt for that Full Moon.

I planned on making the final list within my tree in order to give that extra boost of magic to my intentions list.

The days flew by in a flurry of packing and purging. My home was pretty much empty except for big furniture, cooking supplies, toiletries and clothes.

When my neighbors or friends would come in and see the boxes and packing, the conversation would go something like this:

Them: "I didn't know you were moving!"

Me: "I am."

Them: "Where is your new place?"

Me: "I don't know yet, but I know it's on its way to me."

Them: After a confused look, "Oh...OK. Cool."

I didn't know how to explain to them that I just knew. When I feel things in my bones they happen, and happen it did.

My trip to Humboldt had finally arrived, and I took my journal and drove 11 hours up the I-5 to my soul's home.

I worked on my list the whole time I was up there, really visioning exactly what I wanted and feeling the emotions of being within it, greeting clients at the front door and feeling at peace with enough space for me to grow and spread my beautiful new wings.

My list was quite long and specific, and the musts were:

- 2 Bedrooms
- Hardwood Floors
- Trees and nature around me
- Fireplace
- Character…no boring, boxy house

On the Full Moon I went to my Tree, and read the list to her and spoke to her about how I had been looking, but none of the places I saw were right.

Just at that very moment, my phone rang, and it was my landlord.

Yet another phone call from The Universe received within my tree.

I had become friends with my landlord, so months before I asked her if she had any 2-bedroom places open, as they own a good number of different sized properties in the area. She told me that she did not, but she would let me know if anything came up.

She was now on the phone and I was within my tree, list in hand hearing that one 2-bedroom is available last minute as a woman left without any notice.

She told me that I had to come see it and make a decision soon, or else it would go out to the public and be rented immediately.

I told her I was 700 miles away in a forest, but I was coming back in two days, and I would immediately go see it as soon as I returned.

The moment I walked into it, I knew it was mine.

I felt it in my bones, and I knew which room was my bedroom, and which was calling out to be The Healing Woods. Even though it was in shambles, and half of the woman's stuff was left and trash was thrown around everywhere, the paint was peeling and it was filthy…I saw the potential within, and I knew that I was standing in my next home.

Everything on my list was within this home, with the addition of a beautiful view of the mountains, multiple rose bushes planted in the front and an amazing large mantle above the working fireplace, which is my seasonal altar.

I called my landlord, said yes, and she began with the painting and cleaning, and I moved in the next week.

Thankfully I had spent the past couple months purging and packing, so all I had to do was pack the essentials I had left and rent the U-Haul. I was ready to move.

Of course the moment the contract was signed, and I was given the keys to my new place that was more than double the rent of my tiny hobbit house and four times the size, the fears began.

What am I doing?

Why am I leaving the security of cheap rent?

What if I lose my job?

I have a car payment and double rent now, what if I lost it all?

As soon as I was having those thoughts, I knew I was on the right track, and even though my heart was beating with fear. I knew it was also beating with excitement, and I wasn't going to let my fears make this decision for me. I was in charge of my destiny, and I manifested this within my tree, so it had to be right!

As I was unpacking into my new bigger and better cocoon, I was having difficulty finding a place for my box with twenty five years worth of journals that I carried around with me from house to house.

For the longest time I kept them under my bed, but then once I was attuned to Reiki and more aware of energy, I felt as if all of the pain and darkness within them was filling the very room I was trying to sleep in, and so I moved them to the garage.

Something had changed within me with this move, and I felt as if I needed to cut ties to that depression and rage that filled most of those journals. It was as if I had been lugging around a dead body with me every time I moved with those journals, and now that I had fourteen more years worth. The size of the box they were in literally was the size of a small coffin.

I decided that on New Year's Eve of 2011 going into 2012, I would once and for all burn all of those journals at midnight, and forever cut the emotional and energetic ties to everything I dumped in them.

This night was in fact, a Full Moon, and the perfect place that I have found to bury things that I am completely done with it is The Salton Sea in the desolate salt covered desert of Imperial Valley, California.

I knew that there were some beautiful nuggets of writing within the putrid anger, hatred and depression that was littering those pages, so I took the whole month of December to hermit myself away in my home, and read each page of each journal one by one in chronological order. It was like living the past twenty five years of my life all over again.

The loves, the breakups, the joys, the magic, the fear, the pain, the proclamations that came true, and the ones that seemed as if they never would. I revisited all of it, and kept some of the beautiful nuggets I found in a Word document in case I wanted them for lyrics or to include in a book someday.

I recently unearthed this document, and wanted to share a few of those nuggets with you:

1/1/00
I am what I decide and allow...nothing more...nothing less.

4/16/03
***I'm happy to be poor of pocket, yet rich in soul.
I just need to find happiness within me now...the rarest of diamonds that has ever been unearthed from the deepest cave within my soul.***

5/26/03
Love never happens when you want it to...only when you are ready.

3/22/06
My desire for love has trumped my fear of it.

8/3/06
Love is the easiest thing to fall into, yet the most painful thing to fall out of.

8/12/06
Do not let what has lead you in the past lead you to the past.

5/14/07
It's a delicate dance we are fumbling through…me tipping out my heart and giving it to my delusions of you.

9/22/08
My staples holding the colon resection incision are coming out today. This represents my last stages of healing for this 10-month affliction.
I am finally strong enough to hold myself together.

1/15/09
All of these things are part of the beautiful mosaic of pain which decorates my past. Beautiful strength derived from pain…the hardest strength to come by which sticks with you forever.

4/3/09
No love can grow where only the seeds of lust have been planted.

11/18/09
I love the direction my life is headed because I am finally navigating with my soul instead of my mind.

1/2/10
Nature is terrifyingly beautiful and extremely wise.
It screams lessons out to us, but most humans are so blind and deaf they cannot hear or see what it right in front of them.

4/18/10
My mind tells me to run yet my body begs to linger.

5/6/10
Who is he?
What is he?
Why am I so incredibly drawn to him?
It's like we are two magnets…clinging to each other because there is no other way to go besides further into each other.

3/12/11
He came and went as quickly as a forest fire rushes through the dried up foliage where love and hope once stood.

6/18/11
I need to quit scribbling in journals and start typing my book.

I lugged the dusty box-coffin for the musings of the past quarter century into the trunk of my car, and took off for the desert on New Year's Eve, away from the clubs, away from society and directly into the last free place on earth: Slab City.

Slab City was my place to hide out. I had a life that was very public. I was on stage with the band, in clubs and shows promoting, building a business and surrounded by people constantly at my full-time job too.

Every now and then I needed to disappear and be completely off the grid, and Slab City was one of my hideouts.

It is literally in the middle of nowhere, somewhere close to the Mexican border and The Salton Sea.

The Salton Sea is a dying sea surrounded by thousands of white dried up mummified fish littering the shores.

It was once a sacred lake for the Native Americans called Lake Cahuilla, but the white man decided to redirect the Colorado River, and have farmers' run off dump into this sacred body of water to create seaside property in the middle of the desert.

In the 50s it was booming with fisherman, boating, resorts, family vacations and picnics. Today, after the river was again redirected and severe drought came in, it is desolate, forgotten, eerie, silent and otherworldly.

Among the nothingness of The Salton Sea area is Slab City, which also in the 50s was an active Army Base called Camp Dunlap. Once it was dismantled, people discovered these large slabs of concrete that were left there, and they started camping there, and living off the grid without having to pay any rent.

There is no running water, no trash pick up, no mail service, no electricity, no rent, no police and no rules; it is called the last free place on earth for a reason…you can feel the freedom there, which is why I fell in love with it so deeply.

Today there are art colonies, campers, trailers, teepees, a live music venue called The Range, a library of free books for trade, a church, a pet cemetery, coffee house, houses built out of old water silos, people living off the grid with solar power, gardening, creating art and one of the biggest art colonies in The Slabs called East Jesus.

I first met Container Charlie who created East Jesus on my first trip to The Slabs on New Year's Eve 2007.

I was tired of being in clubs playing with the band or otherwise celebrating New Year's Eve, and that particular New Year's Eve happened to fall on a Blue Moon, so I told myself I would do something I had never experienced before for that particular New Year celebration.

My friend Lisa invited me to Slab City, and my soul said yes, even though my brain had no idea how to even find her there or what it was I was driving three-and-a-half hours into the middle of nowhere to get to…but when I feel things in my bones…I have to do it.

I arrived in the mish mash of trash, art, campers, shade structures and felt an energy that felt so alive and free, which acted as pheromone for someone who felt so trapped in her busy life.

I sang the New Year in on stage at The Range with a band of random Slabbers who played White Rabbit. Singing on that stage in the middle of nowhere on a Blue Moon New Year's Eve night with the white desert shining all around in the bright glow of the moon turned my adventure switch on. I knew that night that I could not continue for too much longer living the split life of a Media Buyer in the Advertising Industry and a Reiki Master who died and came back to this world in order to spread Reiki as far and wide as I possibly could on this planet.

I spent the night freezing my ass off in the 30-something degree night in a beat up extra trailer of some guy my friend introduced me to, writing in my journal by the light of a Road Opener candle and I felt so at home. I knew that I had found someplace special.

That next morning, Lisa and I were walking around exploring, and we found an art garden, which literally shined amongst the piles of rubble and dry desert shrubbery surrounding us.

There was a man in the garden smiling at us, and he invited us in. This was my first introduction to Container Charlie, the art car driving, Burning Man, Mensa member, ex NASA employee, musician, artist and desert recluse.

I later found out he knew people all over the world who turned up for his memorial after he died within the beautiful slice of desert freedom he named East Jesus a few years later.

That day, however, Charlie was very much alive. He invited us into his living quarters, which were like a mansion compared to the places I was hanging out in prior in The Slabs.

He had a recording studio, full kitchen with fridge and stove, multiple semi containers converted into rooms, a huge New York City bus half buried in the ground, multiple art installations everywhere and a grand piano with guitars hooked up and ready to go.

He offered us whiskey and told me he heard me sing at The Range, and that he and I should sing together. We had that beautiful conversation musicians have when they want to jam together trying to figure out which songs both know, and we decided upon a duet called Henry Lee by Nick Cave and PJ Harvey.

I sang my ass off with Charlie, and within music, we became fast friends. Charlie and I kept in touch, and I always went to visit him whenever I was in the Slabs, and I always had a place to stay with him to sing, write, create, hide out and do whatever I had to do.

After my amazing adventures for The Blue Moon New Year celebration, I started calling The New Year the Blue Year instead, and I told myself I would fill that year with new adventures and doing things I was always afraid to do before.

I commemorated The Blue Year by writing lyrics to one of The Darklings' songs and named it "Happy Blue Year":

Happy Blue Year

Song By The Darklings
Lyrics by Kristin Dwan

Desert shores glisten no more,
Under my shoes,
Root of fear…hinder my bloom,
I have yet to lose.

I wash my fear in The Salton Sea,
Mountains of obsidian for me,
Skeletons crack under my feet,
Happy Blue Year to me.

Blood red skies behind my eyes,
Blue Moon rising.
Milky Way guide my way,
Hypnotize me.

I wash my fear in The Salton Sea,
Mountains of obsidian for me,
Skeletons crack under my feet,
Happy Blue Year to me.

After Charlie's untimely death by heart attack a few years later, a man named Frank took over East Jesus, and to this day it is alive and well as a haven to artists to escape the world for as short or as long as they would like.

Frank is about 7 feet tall, and a hitchhiker who was writing a book titled "A Thumb and a Prayer" about all of the angels he had met during his many years on the road.

I called Frank New Year's Eve of 2011, and told him I was coming to burn a bunch of journals, and he said, "Great…I'll get the bonfire ready"

I arrived to a scene of artists, musicians and slabbers sharing food, drink and music, and I made myself at home. That is the beautiful thing about East Jesus: everyone is accepted and celebrated, as long as you are not an asshole.

Right before midnight, I got Frank, and he dragged a king-sized mattress out in the middle of East Jesus and doused it with gasoline. He said, "This should get going enough for all those books you've got!"

With that…he dropped a match on it, and the bed erupted into flames. I watched in awe as the flames rose up taller than me, and with the Full Moon shining down upon us, I grabbed the journals one at a time and threw them into the growing inferno.

I noticed that as the books hit the flames, they opened up as they burned and the pages turned to ash, almost as if the desert and the moon were reading them. I mentioned this to Frank, to which he said, "You've gotta be careful what you ask the desert for. It is always listening, and it will always reply."

Just as he said this, one single page flew up into the air towards the moon, burning on the edges and then turning into a flying ember disappearing into the desert night sky.

This could have been a page filled with pain, loathing, depression…or a lyric, poem, celebration or intention…whatever it was it was gone, and I had released it to the desert for it to answer me.

My adrenalin was coursing as I looked up at the Blue Moon surrounded by the Milky Way where that single page flew up, and I screamed like a warrior, "Did you read that? I'm done with it! It's not mine anymore!!!!"

I felt lighter and lighter as each book was thrown into the flames one by one, the pain within it that I had recorded was being burned away from me, and as each book was thrown in for their demise, I felt more and more alive.

The fire that burned me alive in 1998 didn't even take my prior years of journals, and I lugged them around with me ever since. At that point in 2012 things were changing, and I had changed, and this fire was going to be the one to seal the deal.

I have never forgotten the wise words the desert sage Frank uttered that night, and I have taken them to heart every time I go out into the desert to do any type of ritual working or meditation.

I am very careful what I ask the desert for, because it is always listening, and it definitely has always responded to me.

I returned home from the burn, and I immediately put The Healing Woods on Yelp in order to open myself up to complete and utter strangers finding me online, which was something I was scared to do.

I had always relied on finding clients through word of mouth and friends of friends. It felt safer that way. I was protected in a way from being completely and totally seen in the world.

Well, I was different now, and safety gave way for power to manifest itself within me, and I got The Healing Woods out onto the World Wide Web in as many different places as possible, and because I was ready, and the calls and emails started flooding in.

The five star reviews were appearing on Yelp, and the phone rang more and more often as more and more reviews appeared. I was working 9-5pm at the office and working 5-9pm at The Healing Woods as well as weekends when I didn't have a show to do. Sometimes I was even taking a full day of clients on a Saturday and then spending the night at a club playing a show.

After about six months, I was getting so many calls and e-mails from complete strangers about Reiki and Tarot, that I was closing my door at the advertising agency and taking Healing Woods calls and booking appointments while on the clock.

The Universe was definitely showing me that I was on the right path, and I just needed to keep charging down it.

I felt free and so fulfilled when I was on stage with the band and in The Healing Woods with my clients.

I felt attacked, shackled, stressed and sick to my stomach when I was in the office as a Media Buyer with a sea of toxic people surrounding me.

I was attracting more and more clients, but still not enough to pay my rent, car payment and pay down the thousands of dollars I still had of debt from the fire, DUI and other tragedies in life, so stuck I was in this triple life of Media Buyer, Lead Singer and Reiki Master as long as I could in order to pay the debt down.

As with everything in my life to this point, tragedy was always my wide open door to growth, and tragedy struck again, just as things were heating up for The Healing Woods.

It was shortly after being cut out of my brand new 2012 Toyota Camry by the Jaws of Life, that I discovered Fire Cupping. I have learned many painful lessons from fire in my life and this time, my lifelong dance within its lessons was a healing one instead of a destructive one.

I was T-boned by a woman going 45 mph through a red light right into my driver door.

She was on her way home from Bible Study, while I was heading out of Pagan Choir. The irony of this kills me; you can't make this stuff up.

I suffered cracked ribs and a bruised lung. I didn't even know internal organs could bruise, but within this lesson I felt exactly how painful that feels every time I breathed in, and we have to do that to survive countless times a day.

I was rushed in an ambulance to the ER after they cut me out of the car, and was given many tests and pain pills, which after a week or so, made me feel even worse with constipation and stomach aches.

I couldn't sleep through the night the pain was so bad, and I spent pretty much a month on disability in bed recovering. I asked my doctor what I could do to speed up the recovery, and she said, "Just bed rest and pain medication. It could take up to 4-6 months before you are completely healed."

I do not take in what I am told by doctors as far as how long something will heal. I listen to what they say, and then use my will, Reiki and any holistic medicine I can add into the mix of their western medicine to speed up the process. This has always worked wonderfully for me, and I have a track record of healing in half the time the doctors sentence me with.

During this particular test, I asked The Universe to please bring some healing to me besides the constant Reiki I was doing on myself, acupuncture and the massages that my beautiful friends came and helped me with.

That was when I was invited to go to a healing retreat within the Joshua Tree desert, and I was able to drive by this time, since it had been about a month and a half since the accident. I decided to get out of town for a bit and receive some healing.

It was a bunch of different healers who met at The Joshua Tree Retreat Center for a weekend of trading healing work with each other, and I was there with my Tarot Cards and my hands for Reiki.

I only knew a couple of the girls there, but everyone was amazing, and I really enjoyed the trades I received. This was where I was introduced to Fire Cupping by one of the healers there, Sonya who was an acupuncturist.

She received Reiki from me, and I received my first Fire Cupping session from her, and it was like nothing I had ever experienced in my life. I went to massage school, and I was never even taught about this ancient Chinese modality.

She took locking forceps with cotton dipped in alcohol and lit them on fire with one hand. With the other she held glass cups and put the fire into the cups for a split second, and then put the cups on her patient's back using the suction from the fire.

It looked so alien, and so beautiful and I was immediately drawn to it, and wanted to experience how it felt.

It was like the most intense massage I had ever received, but also the most healing.

For a month I was not able to move the left side of my waist or arm without intense pain from the accident, and after the cupping, I felt the pain lessened, and I had more movement.

Plus the suctioning felt amazing on my back, neck and shoulders which were also very tight from all of the bed rest and different ways I was holding my body due to the pain.

I was hooked on Fire Cupping, and she said she was looking to find a Reiki Master she jived with, and we decided to do a bigger trade of me attuning her to Reiki 1 and her teaching me Ancient Chinese Fire Cupping.

During my lesson, I really took to it, and started making it my own. Sonya said it was almost like I must have been an old Chinese lady in a past life I learned it so quickly.

It was my element, and I was so excited to be able to breathe some life into this ancient art that is all but dead except for Chinatown and certain acupuncturist offices.

Plastic cups, which are easier to work with for the practitioner, have buttons on them you pull to create the suction were created, and hardly anyone bothers to use the fire anymore.

I personally believe the fire is a huge part of the healing, so I took it upon myself to get as well practiced as I could, and the more I practiced, the more I made this ancient Chinese healing art my own by adding in massage and the Japanese healing art of Reiki to the session.

Cupping leaves people very vulnerable and open energetically speaking. They have released toxins, emotions and stuck energies during the session, so I wanted to protect people as they left, so I sealed them off energetically with Reiki before they went back out into the world.

My cupping caught on, and before I knew it, I was being contacted by reality TV shows to be filmed for Cupping, doing internet radio interviews about it, and it took over for my massage clients as I moved further away from bodywork and more deeply into teaching and doing speaking engagements about Reiki.

I was the only person in my area on Yelp who offered Fire Cupping, and after Dr. Oz did a segment about it, my phone went crazy for a few weeks all with calls about Fire Cupping.

With the extra money I was able to make with this beautiful influx of clients, I got very focused on paying off all of my credit card debt, and in October of 2012, I made my last payment on it, and my credit card balance was officially $0!

This was literally the first time in my adult life that I did not have any credit card debt at all. I never thought it would happen. After the fire and all through my 20s and early 30s I had $40, 000 in debt, and as much as I tried to pay it off, the compound interest, car repairs and other unforeseen expenses kept getting in the way.

There were times in my advertising career that I was making over $100,000 a year…but I was living like I was making $20,000 with all of the bills I was trying to pay off.

I was so excited to be able to finally save money now to put into building The Healing Woods, and maybe even rent a space outside of my home, and have a nest egg of money with which to transition slowly into a full time Reiki Master.

The Universe had other plans for me.

To celebrate being debt free for the first time in my life, I invited over some close witch friends of mine for a Samhain Bullshit Bonfire, which basically was us hanging out, drinking some wine, eating some food and burning lists of things we were done with and wanting to walk away from in life within my living room fireplace.

Samhain is the Pagan name for Halloween, it is the day that the veil between the spirit world and earthly realm is the thinnest, so we were also working with our Ancestors and honoring them by creating sugar skulls. Little did I know how potent and powerful my first Bullshit Bonfire for a group of people would be.

I would burn things all the time on my own, lists, pictures, prayers, journals…houses...but never did I invite others to join, but this just felt like a good thing to do in my bones, so of course I did it.

I burned all of my old debt papers, credit card bills and bank statements. I also burned a bunch of stuff about stress at work and at the very end I wrote on my list, "Anything that is in the way of my soul's greatest good."

Two weeks later, I was called into my boss's office and given my last paycheck, and told that it was not my work ethic or anything personal, but the company was going through huge amounts of layoffs, and I was the last buyer to be hired, so I was the first to be let go.

Within my shock, I actually smiled at the room full of my ex bosses, and said, "Right on."

This was definitely a huge sign from The Universe that it was time for me to take a leap of faith, and to build my business and soul's work instead of running blindly to another job.

Of course, with my decision to build my business up and get real about making a good enough living to pay all of my monthly bills with it, I had to have complete focus on The Healing Woods.

I came to the sad realization that my days as the lead singer of The Darklings were numbered, and after half a year of trying to do both, it proved to be too much.

I had to make the hard decision of leaving a dying band I still had passion for to build a sprouting business I had soul connection to.

For the first time in twelve years, I was no longer in a band.

For the first time in over twenty years I was not planning on being employed by any job.

For the first time ever I was standing on the biggest cliff I had ever been on ready to take a leap of faith into entrepreneurship.

YOUR
HEALING ACTION!

Please log onto
www.thehealingwoods.com/book-bonus/
in order to access your next bonus to further
your own personal journey of igniting
your light within!

CHAPTER 9

FIRE CUPPING, BULLSHIT BONFIRES AND USUI'S HOLY FIRE REIKI

Some Women Are Lost In The Fire.
Some Women Are Built From It.

— Michelle K.

The year was 2013. I was free and for the first time in my life, I owned my time and energy.

I didn't have to plan vacations around a 9-5 schedule and get written permission from a boss to go into nature for a week. In fact, I could leave for a month instead of a week if I wanted to in order to connect with my beloved redwoods. There was no one to ask permission of in life except me.

It was the most exciting point in life, but also one of the scariest times in life.

The first Monday I awoke without an alarm clock and without the need to run out of bed and get my shower started to race out the door to get to work on time, I laid there for a while, and enjoyed what it felt like to not have to be anywhere I didn't want to be.

I slowly rose out of bed after petting my purring kitties Anika and Amma, and closed my eyes to give thanks and gratitude to The

Universe for this beautiful restart button in life.

I made a post on Facebook that I was now running The Healing Woods full time, and that I was free to see people M-F 10am until 8pm, and weekends as well. I sent Reiki to that post before I posted it with the intention that the right people would read it, and also as a sign to The Universe that I was ready, willing and able to run The Healing Woods full time and become a full time healer.

My friends were amazingly supportive, and before I knew it, I had a full week of clients on the books within a few hours of that post.

Ask and ye shall receive. I would also like to add: believe and ye shall receive.

This was a huge "shit or get off the pot" moment within my life, and I decided that I was going to do as many things as I could to put myself within the energy of abundance and success even though there were some people around me who were within fear when it came to me building my business.

My parents were as supportive emotionally as they could be, but they come from a different era, the era that teaches you to start a career, create stability and hold on for dear life until you retire.

So obviously once I told them that I was going to build a Reiki business instead of pounding the pavement for a new job, there were a lot of questions that came up for them. The first one being, "What is Reiki?"

My business was a slow but steady build, and one practice that I had was kissing every check, dollar bill and online payment that came my way with love, gratitude and excitement.

At this point in my life, I had a long love affair with debt, and we had just broken up before this new relationship with flow started up, so I wanted to alert The Universe to the fact that I am open to the beautiful energetic flow of money coming to me through my soul's work.

My whole life I struggled with control issues. I tried to control things in my ad agency jobs, and that was a huge joke. I tried to control things in love, and that always backfired in my face, and in the beginning I felt like I had to be in control with building my business, and I quickly learned that although I had to be completely present and grounded in order to run this healing business, I also needed to be able to flow within it instead of direct.

I absolutely loved the beautiful places my heart flowed me to once I took the reins from my head.

One of my favorite ways to turn off my head was to be in nature and meditate. I started a practice which I still have today where once a week I go somewhere within nature. The forest is my place of grounding within that earth element womb. With my work being in Reiki energy, which has a way of taking me out of my body, I really need that true connection with the planet I live on fairly regularly.

The ocean is my place to give hard emotional things to that I can't seem to clear myself of on my own. That amazing water element of Mama Ocean literally cleansing me from head to toe, and even pushing me around to shake me up within her powerful waves when needed.

The desert is where I go in order to connect to the air element, feeling and hearing the beautiful song of the desert winds, wide open spaces all around me and the huge expansiveness the desert brings really shows me the wide open roads around me, and landscapes of possibility as far as the eye can see.

The element of fire I connect to easily within my own home. That element is within me always, it had literally been burned into me early on, and I honor her by burning candles, incense and lists of intentions within my fireplace in my own living room.

Anytime I am within nature it is pretty much a given that I am going there to meditate and connect, and when I am meditating, I am connecting to Reiki, which in turn connects me to my Reiki Guides.

One of the bonuses of being attuned to any level of Reiki is that Reiki comes with these beautiful beings called Reiki Guides to help you along your path.

My Reiki Guides were pretty silent for the first 2 levels of my attunements, but once I was attuned to be a Reiki Master, they started talking, and when they talk…I listen. Especially when it doesn't make sense to my head.

Within a meditation on a very special Full Moon, my Reiki Guides showed me a vision of me getting re-attuned to be a Reiki Master again, even though I had been a Reiki Master for many years.

This was one of those messages from my guides that made no sense at all to my head, but I felt in my bones, so of course I logged onto The International Center for Reiki Training (ICRT) website, and booked my class.

Since one of my goals this lifetime is to bring Reiki into hospitals as a trusted form of treatment to patients especially pre and post surgery, I decided that getting my re-attunement to Reiki Master from this center would look more official than the private Reiki Masters I received my other attunements with.

At the time, I was in the system of City of Hope Cancer Center as a volunteer in the Spiritual Care Unit trying my hardest to get them to change their mind about allowing Reiki on a volunteer basis. They had people passing around Eucharistic Sacrament and reading Bible passages to patients, but when it came to offering Universal Light Energy to patients, the powers that be were not open.

Reiki cannot harm, it is a pure energy that helps the body's systems function at their best, and works beautifully to strengthen the immune system, which is almost mandatory for Cancer treatment.

I also added into my Reiki Tool Belt a class in Oncology Reiki, and learned many amazing ways to help strengthen Cancer patients as they go through the horrific treatments that they have to survive in order to fight this debilitating disease.

I was excited for my upcoming Reiki Master Class with ICRT, and was using my Oncology certification quite regularly within my Healing Woods practice, but unfortunately not within the fortress of City of Hope unless it was while being hired by my own clients while they were patients there.

The morning of my re-attunement to Reiki Master, I showed up to the class walking on air.

There were people from all over the world in my class including a woman from Egypt and a woman from the United Kingdom.

I loved the diversity of the class, and was so excited to learn from a prestigious school of Reiki such as the ICRT was.

My newest Reiki Master called the class to order, and said the following words which still give me chills to this day, "I want to welcome all of you and congratulate you on being the first class to learn and be attuned to Usui's Holy Fire Reiki."

All other sounds in the room disappeared, and I kept hearing the word "Fire" echoed over and over again, and I remembered my Reiki guides calling me to get re-attuned right then and the emotions of all of that overtook me and I started balling right in the middle of class.

My Reiki Master asked me what was happening with me, and I told the class all about my beginnings with Reiki coming from being burned alive, and how beautiful it was that my Reiki Guides called me to be re-attuned right now within the first Holy Fire Reiki class.

After I told my story, other students were crying, and my Reiki Master was silent for a bit. Then she said, "We are called to the fire when it is time to shine."

Truer words were ever spoken to me within a class.

For those readers who do not know anything about the history of Reiki or who or what Usui is, I will explain a bit here.

In the early 1900's, Dr. Mikao Usui in Japan truly believed that there was more to healing people than medicines and surgeries, so he went on a three-week fasting meditation on top of Mt. Kurama, with the intention of getting Divine guidance on how to take healing to a deeper level.

On the last day of his meditation, the Reiki Symbols and the wisdom of how to attune others to Reiki energy was bestowed upon him, and from there it grew all throughout Japan and spread to the US, UK, Australia, Canada and by now, most countries in the world have people within them practicing some form of Reiki energy medicine.

Today, if you Google the word Reiki you will find close to a hundred different types of Reiki. Some are offshoots of Usui's Reiki like Karuna Reiki, Reiki Ryoho and Holy Fire Reiki.

Some are Tibetan, some Japanese and some have been downloaded most likely by people high on hallucinogens and put onto the web like Fairy Reiki and Alien Reiki.

As energetic and in the ether as I can be doing Reiki as a full time job, I always like to know that the energy I am working with has its roots in the Usui System of Natural Healing, which has its roots in the first Reiki that was discovered on Mt. Kurama by Dr. Usui himself.

Truth be told, I believe Universal Light Energy, which Reiki is comprised of, has been around far before Usui, and that Jesus was a Reiki Master, and before him, I believe Ancient Egypt had its form of Reiki, as well.

Throughout history there have been accounts of laying on of hands healing, and since humans, plants and animals are all made up of energy; it is very believable that energy would heal all of us on a very deep level.

Once The Holy Fire Energy was ignited within me, life took some huge shifts, beginning with my dream world.

The night I became a Holy Fire Reiki Master, I had another one of those dreams that felt so real. It felt as if I was traveling within another level of existence, and I felt, heard, tasted and smelled everything happening within it.

The dream started out showing me a dark and stormy night. Purple flashes of lightning colored the black sky and the cold wind blew my hair all over the place.

Six of my Reiki Guides dressed in purple-hooded robes were leading me through the darkness to a huge black mountain on the horizon. As we neared the mountain, I notice a crack towards the bottom, and we walked into the pitch black of the crack. Just as we entered the mountain, torches of purple fire lead our way down a hallway.

I felt safe, because I knew I was with my Reiki Guides, but the scenery I was traveling through was quite nightmarish.

We turned a corner within the tunnel, and into a beautiful cavern with a huge stone sacrificial altar inside of it. Dragon's Blood incense was wafting through the air, and purple candles with purple flames were flickering all around the altar.

My Reiki Guides motioned for me to jump on the altar, and I did so without question or fear.

One approached me with a huge axe and put my arms stretched out before me with my hands on a chopping block. Still, I was unafraid.

He chopped each hand off completely. I felt and heard the bones of my wrists crack, and watched as the blood spilled everywhere onto the altar. Not afraid, even still.

I looked at the nubs I had where my hands used to be, and I noticed a glow of white light coming towards me out of the corner of my eye. One of my guides was carrying two beautiful hands made of light. As he placed these new hands of light onto me, he said, "With your new hands you will heal on the soul level. Never forget the darkness your soul encountered in order to ignite the light within."

And with that, I was awake with my heart beating out of my chest and tears in my eyes.

The moment my eyes fluttered open, and I was completely awake. I saw the image of one of my guides still in my room for a split second. He was surrounded by light, and his hood was off, so I could see his face.

He had the face of a beautiful Japanese man whose eyes were smiling into me with the purest love I have ever felt besides that of my mother. He looked so proud of me, and with a huge smile on his face he bowed to me with his hands in Gassho position, otherwise known as Prayer Position, over his heart.

Until then, I had never actually seen a spirit or guide in this dimension unaltered.

I have sensed guides, seen them within my third eye and imagined what they might look like, but here he was bright as day, and I was completely sober and awake.

The next Full Moon following my ignition into Holy Fire Reiki, I was visited not only by My Reiki Guides…but also by Amma.

In this very real feeling dream, I was in the arms of Amma receiving Darshan, and as she was embracing me, she sang into my ears. I was instantly transported to my Reiki Guides again in the purple hooded cloaks.

They again bowed to me as I entered the cave, and I then noticed they all had glowing white hands of light like the ones they gave to me the last time I saw them.

One came up to me, and touched my third eye with his glowing white finger of light, and I physically felt a shock run through my whole body. As his finger was resting on my third eye, he said, "So you can see all of the beauty your healing work brings to this world."

Again, I awoke in a sweat with my heart pounding out of my chest, and this time I cried tears of joy, because these dreams were coming to speak for The Universe to let me know that I was 100-percent on the right path.

After my attunement to Holy Fire Reiki, I noticed that the types of clients I was attracting changed as well.

In all of my years of practicing Reiki, it always seemed as if I would get certain types of clients all at once, and it was usually clients who were going through something that I had worked through myself.

In the beginning, it was people who were fighting severe depression, and even ones grappling with suicidal thoughts and attempts.

I am always the first to say that no one should forego the help of a doctor or licensed therapist when they are dealing with a severe diagnosis either mentally or physically. Reiki is not meant to replace medical treatment, it is meant to enhance it.

I had one woman in particular who was diagnosed as bipolar, and her first time coming to see me, I had to have the curtains drawn, no music on whatsoever and she asked me to speak very slowly and softly, because she couldn't handle a lot of intrusion and talk.

We spoke slowly and softly in the dark and silent room, and I met her exactly where she was, because I had been there, and knew exactly what she was feeling. She really enjoyed her first session, and booked again a few weeks later.

After she received a few sessions here and there, we were able to turn soft music on, and speak about some deeper subjects, because she knew she was safe and able to confide in me.

She began a weekly package with me and continued to see and feel amazing results. She then felt strong enough to want to take on learning Reiki, so she could do it on herself in between sessions with me.

With each level of attunement she received with Reiki, she became brighter and more balanced in her emotions and at one point, she told me that she had even been working with her doctors on lowering her medications.

I am so happy and proud to say that this scared girl who came to me years ago needing complete darkness and silence within her sessions is now a thriving Reiki Master who is specializing in helping women who have suffered child abuse. That was the root of her own personal darkness, and she is now able to help them through their healing because she knows what worked for her, and can share that wisdom and healing with them.

After helping a flood of people with depression, I started to attract a bunch of Oncology patients who were battling Cancer.

So many, that I decided to take a special class in Oncology Reiki to learn about Cancer, how it begins, how it spreads and how to work with people during Cancer Treatments.

Never will I tell an Oncology patient that Reiki will cure their Cancer, but what I will tell them is that Reiki will help treat their spirit and emotions through the intense treatments their body is going through.

Reiki will lift the spirits of that person, strengthen the immune system and help give them a time that is all about them receiving instead of their lives constantly being fighting this disease.

I have worked on people inside City of Hope as they are receiving treatments and I have seen some get a clean bill of health and am the first one giving them big hugs at their "Fuck Cancer" parties.

I have also been there giving Reiki to a dear friend in the walls of City of Hope as he took his final labored breath once he was taken off of a breathing machine. I felt his spirit pass through my hands and fill up that whole entire room. I felt his freedom from Cancer, his release and his deep love for the room full of family and friends who were all there with him as he passed.

We should all be so lucky to have that much love in the room when we pass.

I never have been diagnosed with Cancer, but I did have a scare that was within the same ballpark.

In 2012, I was getting a full blood panel done, and the doctor gave me the bad news that I tested positive for Hepatitis C. This is the big one. The one that has no cure, and the one that I was told, usually leads to liver Cancer.

I had done lots of drugs in my youth, but never using any needles, so I was in shock with this diagnosis, that usually comes from dirty needles. I didn't use dirty needles, but I sure had a lot of blood transfusions in the Burn Ward, in the 90's before they were under more strict regimens, so I am almost positive that is where I contracted it.

The doctors immediately wanted to shoot me up with vaccines for Hepatitis A and B, and told me that taking Interferon was the next step in treatment, depending upon how high the viral load was in my blood.

I did some research on Interferon, and the side effects range from Flu-like symptoms, major depression and suicidal thoughts and actions. I was told I would have to inject myself daily with this for a year.

I may not have had Cancer ever, but I could definitely empathize with someone who did as far as the fear of intense medical treatment and having an "incurable disease" goes. I went through a bit of a depression right after learning all of this, and after I allowed myself some time to feel that, I sprang into action and did my research on other ways of treating Hep C.

I learned that I should refuse all injections until they do the viral load blood test because the virus within the vaccine shots can cause it to shoot up, thus causing a fake high count, so I refused. Upon my refusal, my doctor actually asked me, "Do you really want to die? I am trying to help you live with these injections."

"Then I will allow them after we do the viral load count, if it shows I still need them." was my response.

I spent a full week before my viral load blood test doing hard core Reiki on myself, having healings sent from others, having acupuncture and having some intense tear-filled talks with The Universe.

There is only a ten percent chance that a body will be able to kick out Hepatitis C without treatment, and I was holding onto that 10 percent with all of my hope and energy.

I took my test, and a couple days later, the doctor called me to tell me that my viral load was zero, that I only had antibodies of Hep C left in my blood and I would need no further treatment.

Again, I raised my tear streaked face to The Universe, and thanked it for the healing through this.

I am completely convinced that all of my years of having Reiki flow through me is what saved me from Hep C. Perhaps it was the healing I received from The Universe itself in the burn ward. Perhaps it was doing Reiki for decades and as a full time job for 5 years...whatever it was, it got me through, and I am still clear to this day.

The next group of clients who were called to me for Reiki were women who were having problems getting pregnant or keeping a baby full term.

I had so many women coming to me wanting desperately to become mothers, and through the trifecta of making Reiki, Chinese Herbs and Acupuncture a regular part of their treatment, nine out of ten women became pregnant.

These women, once getting pregnant, requested that I join them in the hospital as part of their birth team, so I heard the call of The Universe, and took classes on how to be a Birth Doula, did Prenatal Massage and also worked with the mothers and babies postpartum to help with bonding and balancing of hormones for the mama.

I was spending so much time in birthing wards, home births and birth centers that I started a whole separate business for six years called The Reiki Doula.

Once Holy Fire came, I also noticed that people who were not local to me were starting to reach out. I came to terms with the fact that being a Doula was taking over The Healing Woods, and as much as I truly loved being a part of the magical moment when a baby takes its first breath on its own, I saw how full time being a Doula really is.

The due date is really a due month, because the babies will come when they are ready. It could be two weeks before or two weeks after that date, and I started to get one to two births a month, which meant I had to be on call at all hours of the day or night to drop everything and get to that mama to support her during her birth for anywhere from 12-24 hours at a time.

I knew that I wanted to focus more on working with people all over the world and traveling while doing it. I also had a deep passion for empowering other healers and readers to be able to do their soul's purpose of healing full time instead of in between day jobs. I had a long talk with The Universe and my Reiki guides, and asked them to bring to me healers from all over the world who needed help building their business.

I was also open to working with people all over the world for Reiki, Akashic Records reading and Tarot reading as well. Reiki can be sent across oceans to people who need it, and readings can be done from distance as well.

My virtual clients feel like they are in the room with me as we meet on Skype or FaceTime, where we get to connect and look at each other throughout the session. I now have friends and clients all over the United States and in many other countries like Japan, Canada, the UK and Ireland that I met through The Healing Woods.

I feel so blessed to be able to spread this beautiful energy far across the world within the distance Reiki sessions I do, and in the past five years of doing this full time, I learned one huge lesson; this whole world needs all the healers it can get!

Even though my childhood dream was to heal the world, as an adult I now realize that I cannot do it alone. No one can.

This world needs multiple armies of healers out there spreading the light to counteract the armies of destruction in full force.

We have now graduated from Light Workers to Light Warriors, and I am so honored to be the Business Coach for Healers and Mystics who not only understands the numbers, marketing and systems part of building a business, but also the virtue, healing and values part of it.

I provide business coaching for healers by a healer.

When most healers take a class and get certification for a new modality, they are wished luck, and told to work with their spirit guides.

I love my spirit guides, and they are extremely important to me, but they did not build my business. I had to do that.

Most healing classes do not include how to build your practice, and that is where I come in. With my fifteen years in the corporate world making millions for other people, I learned a thing or two about business building, marketing, finding new business and client service.

As a healer and reader of twenty eight years, I also know a thing or two about cutting cords to blockages with receiving, clearing fear and helping build a person from the roots up on the inside.

The regular cookie cutter business coaching does not work for a healer.

I've spent tens of thousands of dollars on my own personal business coaching for The Healing Woods, and I see what cookie cutter one to many coaching lacks.

I am happy to provide laser focused business coaching for healers one-on-one. Each healer's journey to doing this work is as diverse and special as their business is.

Each healer comes with their own blockages, their own talents, their own vision and they deserve to be met one-on-one to walk this journey with a healer who has successfully forged a path to the destination they crave: to be a successful full time healer.

It is time that we all rise up.

The world is literally dying for healers.

We are here to serve the world, and to receive for our service.

I view The Universe as my business partner, and it has not let me down since I took that leap. Whoever is guided to work with me, and says yes to their healing has ended up being the perfect client for me. I literally feel love and pride for my clients as I see them reach goals, and celebrate their victories with them.

I am also there for the darkness and fear that can creep in. I know the darkness just as well as I know the light, and I wouldn't be who I am today without my shadow.

Even though I am in an amazingly strong place now, I am human and my ego can call the voices of fear to creep in now and again. These were the same voices telling me that practicing my soul's purpose of Reiki full time would not last.

I went through a huge stage of fear when I first made the leap of faith to do this work full time. I had those same voices of fear that everyone does, and those voices know well, how to take over out of nowhere.

There were times the voices taunted me with, "You're doing well now, but it won't last." and "Who are you to build a full-time healing practice when you have so much to heal on yourself?" and the ever lovely, "Clients are coming now, and your bills are paid this month, but next month is a different story. What if they all never come back?"

Over and over these fears whispered in my head, but I made conscious decisions to think the exact opposite thoughts, and asked for The Universe to show me what my purpose was.

The Reiki guide dreams and the constant flow of clients calling and e-mailing me through these years provided me with the biggest green light I have ever received to go forward as a Full Time Reiki Master. I knew I had to continue spreading the healing, wisdom and love of Reiki one session, class, speaking engagement and Bullshit Bonfire at a time.

"What exactly is a Bullshit Bonfire?" you ask?

Well, you are about to be guided on how to do one of your very own when you receive your bonus for this chapter!

YOUR HEALING ACTION!

Please log onto www.thehealingwoods.com/book-bonus/ in order to access your next bonus to further your own personal journey of igniting your light within!

CHAPTER 10

MY ACTUAL CONFIRMATION WITH GOD

God is love, and love can get so big that it can cover everybody in the world. If you'll let it.

— Leonard Knight of Salvation Mountain

How does one even begin to put into mere words what the Creator of the Universe is? It is almost impossible.

I have spent my whole life seeking the truth about my Creator, and I am happy to say that in the past decade of the four I have been around, I truly do feel I have found my own truth.

My truth is just that: Mine.

I am not saying mine is the only truth, and it may not be the truth for you, but this book has been all about my spiritual path from Catholicism to Wicca to Kabbalah to Hindu and everything else in between, so of course it must end with the truths I have found around God.

My truths are not given to me via any written book nor by a religion, they are taken from life experience and gnosis I have received through the many wonders of nature given to humans to learn from.

There are certain things that I have grown to know that God is not.

God is not here to judge us. Judging is the job of humans and their egos.

God is completely OK with whatever we choose to do or be. In fact, whatever our mind focuses on comes to be within the world around us.

As above so below and as within so without.

We are each tiny offshoots of God, and have the power to create whatever we want in life. The good, the bad and the visionary.

It took me almost eighteen years of truly getting basically everything I have ever thought of...my hopes and dreams, and yes...even some of my fears to show me that I, as well as all humans, do have a direct connection to the Divine.

Some of us choose to call home daily within prayer and meditation...some only when the shit hits the fan, but all are heard, even when we are not meaning to make that call.

When I was a child, I heard, saw and felt God within nature, and never within the confines of the Catholic church where His name was sung out, windows cascaded multi-colored shadows of his likeness and where the Bible was read with such conviction by priests ordained to be the giver of His truth.

The moon taught me beauty, the ocean taught me about emotions, the forest about healing and the desert about new beginnings and silence. Fire taught me about rebirth and fighting for my life.

The loudest of truths were silently screamed to me from my soul within meditations, and all that I ever needed to get me through the worst in life came from my blood, sweat and tearstained inner Bible called faith.

Faith to me is something different than what I was taught in catechism.

Faith is knowing and allowing what is your highest good to grow out of your very being. The essence of God is inside each and every one of us. We just have to get out of our own way, in order to let it shine.

This is a lot more believable, once you become completely aware of all that you are calling into your world, and owning the good and the bad. Unlike religion, which gives all of our power away to the Underworld bringing evil to the earth and Heaven bringing miracles...we are but bystanders of these man-made ideas controlling our world and our destiny.

God does not control our destiny...only we can do that.

This truth is easy to own when things are good, and can be hard when things are falling apart around us.

When the latter is happening, and we feel completely out of control of anything happening to us - this is when faith comes to play.

Trust in the process of what you have created. Even when what you have created seems to be tearing you down to the very roots of your existence.

Have faith in the emergence of your true strengths and powers to get you through what looks to be the worst thing in the world to ever have happened to you.

Knowing that you will get through it creates that very truth in your life. It allows you to flow through the rebirth of who you can be after who you were washes away. All of this will ebb and flow with your strength as you endure the tides of your creation.

Our lives are like the ocean, and we are the rocks being slowly tumbled on the shore to a beautifully smooth perfection. Without the presence of the waves, there would be no tumbling, and without the tumbling, our true colors and beauty within would not show through.

Tumbling is a slow and steady process, as is creating the life that we want.

Transformation is not something we can just become with a thought. It starts with a thought and a goal, but only comes to the surface after we allow multiple levels of change to lead to the transformation.

Change is easy. We can change our minds in a second, change our clothes in a minute and even change our names, but true transformation takes energy, dedication and patience.

My path from prisoner to master was a long and windy one filled with decades of transformation; definitely not just a change of my mind. It did, however begin with a shift of my mind, and patience and determination as I moved towards my goals.

Another thing God is not is something to fear.

He has given each and every one of us the same chance on earth to live a life, and create whatever we want with it.

Some people create empires, while others create prisons, and everything in-between.

One life is no better than the other, they are completely 100-percent exactly what they are supposed to be. How it changes depends on how we change, and how our perception of who we are changes based on how it feels to live the life we have created.

When I was in my teens, I created a perfect prison for my heart and soul.

I hated love, hated myself and hated God, so of course I was angry, depressed and in so much pain I didn't know what to do with myself. When people are in that much pain, the idea of ending it all is sometimes the only way we feel we can escape that pain.

I believe happiness and anger are a choice we make.

Even within the desperate embrace of suicidal thoughts and actions, I still felt the strain because deep down inside I knew it was not my time to leave this earth. I was just releasing some of the pain and hatred that had built up inside of me over my two decades of tumultuous life.

Once that was released, and left to fend for myself in the psych ward's system, I learned that there were other tools that I could use to release this pain and anger other than razors, safety pins and hot lighters.

I finally chose to look towards the light, and move away from the darkness.

I also believe that spiritual learning comes in layers.

Of course there had to be that moment in time where I wanted to end it all in order to show me the depth of my sadness and hopelessness. Bringing me back to that pain full circle a decade later where I was literally fighting to stay alive in the worst pain I have ever experienced.

That pain woke me up. Its roots run deeply in this earth to hold me steady on my course of building my empire on top of the roots of pain that woke me up to the empire's very existence!

If it were not for the pain I have felt in life, I do not believe I would be the powerful phoenix in life that I am today. I do believe I would still be asleep within the very edges of my pain instead of thrown into the shark infested waters of my pain to feel my way out of it.

Too often we feel the edges of pain, and shy away from it. We don't think we have the power to get through it, so we go into avoidance.

We think of something else, self-medicate, check out or find a beautiful home within denial about whatever it is that festers at the roots of our pain.

Instead of shying away from the tip of the pain that has its dagger pointed at your heart, lean into that pain, and allow the dagger to fully penetrate your heart and exit out your back. Only then will you be completely through the pain.

Only then will it really be behind you, and not just buried within you.

The best way to get over something is to go through it as the saying goes. Get to the heart of the pain, for the lesson of the pain is at the heart. It is as if the heart of the pain speaks directly to your heart, and only then are you allowed passage through it.

On the other side of pain is power, and when we are empowered with our own pain, we are invincible because we only call to us what we are meant to endure, and once we do, the strength we gain will get us to the next lesson.

Speaking of lessons: not all lessons have to be learned within pain either.

It took me some time to learn that. I had such an ironclad wall of hate built up around my heart while I was a prisoner of my own pain, that it took a fire and pain of epic proportions to melt the wall down around me.

Thankfully those walls are gone, as is the prison as a whole, and I have fully stepped into my role as Empress of my Empire of Love in my 40's.

Only now, fifteen years later, do Ambika's Sagely words during that life changing psychic reading make sense to me. She told me point blank that I was a fairy that made the brave decision to come back to earth to teach people about love. It makes sense now because I finally realize that I AM love.

So are you.

So is everyone on this planet.

It is just hard to realize that through so much fear and doubt that we put ourselves through needlessly, which is where the amazing gift of Reiki, comes in.

In all of my years as a Reiki Master, I have seen so many different faces of God come to visit during attunements.

I have seen gods and goddesses such as Odin, Hecate and Brigid come for my pagan clients.

Yemaya and Chango come for my clients within Santeria, Buddha and Quan Yin come for my Buddhist clients and different archangels come in for those studying Kabbalah.

I have even had Jesus, Mary and Christ come for those within the Christian and Catholic faiths...all are welcome within Reiki, and all have come to speak to those who needed to see them in order to feel the huge connection to the Divine that Reiki is.

A while back a minister of the Christian faith contacted me, because he wanted to deepen his connection to Jesus, and was drawn to Reiki in order to experience this.

He first dipped his toe in the water with a session, and felt a huge opening and connection to the energy.

Right after his first session, he booked his Reiki 1 class with me, and we began together on the path of deeper Divine connection via Reiki.

I truthfully was a bit nervous, as I had never attuned an actual minister to Reiki before. I had attuned many Agape Practitioners, and had Jesus come through for them, but this was different.

This was the closest to the priests of my past that didn't understand me at all that I had gotten in my travels with Reiki, and it brought up some old stuff for me.

Through the year that I was working with him, we had many discussions about God, Jesus and Reiki. I was very open about being a witch, and he was very open about hearing my take on God.

We spent a lot of time talking about the Divine and what we felt about it, and surprisingly enough...it was the same exact thing.

My classes I teach are private one-on-one trainings, because Reiki is a soul deep wisdom, and I find it is better to connect with one person at a time to teach them Reiki in the way which is best for them to learn.

Some people want to learn it to heal past traumas such as rapes, deaths of loved ones or miscarriages.

These are all extremely personal transitions in life, which require privacy for them to release what they need to within the training, and receive any healing from me that needs to happen in order to get through the journey of each class.

Most people would not feel comfortable expressing these deep dark hurts in a class of strangers, so I specialize in mentoring people privately to allow them to go as deeply as they need to within the class.

Some people want to use it within birth and death, and since I have been both a Birth Doula as well as a Death Doula focused on Reiki within the transition, I am able to help them specifically with these beautiful tools within their practice.

Some people feel the calling so deeply, they know their soul was put on this planet to do Reiki full time and build a business doing it. I am there for them as well, giving business building tips and am also available to them after their training as their Business Coach to make sure their dream of being a full time abundant Reiki Master is a reality.

I serve students everywhere from people in the sex industry to Ministers within the church, and everyone in between. Reiki does not judge and neither does God in all of the many faces he shows himself to be to these beautiful people from all walks of life.

My classes I took were all filled with people, and I didn't get the one-on-one training I give my students. I know how it feels to not want to ask a question, because you are afraid it is stupid or a waste of time. I know how it feels to be left to practice amongst the other students because one of the students had a huge emotional release and the teacher had to take them into another room and tend to them.

I know how weird it feels to be so emotionally and energetically vulnerable and open amongst strangers, and I do not want to put my students through that. I want them feeling safe to bare all and allow the energy to come in and take them as deeply as they are willing to go into whatever pain they need to release.

When my minister student was attuned to Reiki 1, one of the most beautiful things happened.

He came out of the attunement crying, and took a while to come back 100-percent from the deep experience he just had. Once he was grounded, I asked him how it went.

He looked at me and said, "In all of the years I have studied the Bible and even within my Seminary schooling, this attunement was by far the closest to God that I have ever felt."

I received the most amazing blast of chills hearing that, and cried too. I could not even believe what I was hearing, yet I know it was true because I may not have gone to Seminary school proper, but I did put myself through decades of studying God and his many faces, and I felt the same exact way about Reiki.

After his Reiki 1 attunement, he was on the fast track to Reiki

Master, and went through all 3 levels of training with me. I am proud to know that he has since started his own Reiki business, and is out there bringing this beautiful energy to people of the Christian faith.

My hope is that at one point it can make its way into the church, because as both he and I agreed...Jesus was one of the most amazing Reiki Masters ever.

God cannot be contained within one person's truth, book or religion.

That which has created us is bigger than any idea, awareness or story on this planet. God is multidimensional and omnipresent within every ocean breeze, last dying breath and first scream of life.

I've seen and felt God in many places...church never being one of them.

I felt God in my room the night the flames took over. He was with me as I slept, and worked through my cat to wake me up. He was there as I jumped through the wall of flames to get me out of there alive. Burnt, but alive...burned alive.

I feel God when I light a candle, Bullshit Bonfire or even just my fireplace. Meditating on the dancing likeness of God the flames are and listening to the wisdom this powerful element has to give.

I feel God when I see the Full Moon glowing brightly above, casting shadows amongst the blue light surrounding me. I see God in the hair thin crescent of the New Moon showing the beginning of what is to come for us magically, if we get to know her.

I feel God when I see a shooting star as an answer to a deep and burning question within me, and smile up at the sky and say, "Thank you." every time.

I feel God when I wander around the woods, and hear a raven speak to me, hear the deep flutter of the hawk's wings in the deafening silence or see a dew soaked heart shaped clover glistening in the filtered sunlight of a redwood forest.

I feel God when I am floating in the ocean and a warm current flows in to hug me, a seal floats by and I find a heart shaped rock right in my path after singing my mantra to the sea.

I feel God when I meditate near my ancestor altar and smell my grandmother's perfume, see a vision that turns out to be an answer and hear the laughter of my grandfather warm my soul.

I feel God when I look into the bright with wonder eyes of a newborn the first time they open and also as I gaze into the wise old eyes of a person making the transition into the afterlife.

I hear God within the desert breezes that blow away my worries and whisper wisdom directly to my heart and soul.

I see God within my many teachers this lifetime through countless traditions, imparting to me the many layers of multifaceted wisdom I needed, in order to make my own decision as to who or what my truth about God is.

I feel God within me when a stranger walks into The Healing Woods and hugs me as a friend after their session, telling me they feel lighter and are inspired to believe in themselves and make steps towards their dreams no matter what their fears or pain have told them.

I see God in action at Bullshit Bonfires when a group of strangers gather and read lists of pain, heartache, fear and doubts to each other only to hear that everyone in the room is releasing the same stuff. The tears turning into laughter, and the excitement of the flames burning their blockages away.

I hear God in music, and when I allow my head to turn off and my heart to turn on through my voice. Singing the words I write and hearing melodies within nature to mantra with.

I see God in me...I see God in you...I feel God everywhere and within everyone, and that is how I know I have found my own truth with God.

The only truth that matters in life.

Being a clear channel of Divine energy everyday strengthens this truth within me.

Hope of a connection to God is fragile when given to you by others...faith is unshakable when your truth is born from within.

May your journey lead you to your truth, and I send many blessings to you on your path.

I would love to hear about your story, and how reading this book has inspired you on your journey.

Just reach out to me at www.thehealingwoods.com or send me an e-mail at kristin@thehealingwoods.com.

Yours within the light,
~Kristin Dwan/Reiki Master Mentor

YOUR
HEALING ACTION!
Please log onto
www.healingwoods.com/book-bonus/
in order to access your last bonus to complete
your own personal journey of igniting
your light within!

ABOUT THE AUTHOR

Kristin Dwan is a world renowned Reiki Master and Business Coach for Healers who brings people peace from the first breath of life to the last. She has helped babies come into the world as a Birth Doula and held and comforted people as they took their last breath as a Death Doula.

As a business coach, she guides healers to live their soul's purpose full time instead of in between day jobs. She guides you to awaken within you the healing and wisdom that is yours to use to better your life and the lives around you.

Over the past 25 years, Kristin has helped thousands of healers, spiritual teachers, doctors, scientists and all types people in pain all over the world receive the peace of healing and coaching through Tarot and Reiki.

Made in the USA
Middletown, DE
30 June 2019